Eleanor Cecilia Donnelly

Out of Sweet Solitude

Eleanor Cecilia Donnelly

Out of Sweet Solitude

ISBN/EAN: 9783743305106

Manufactured in Europe, USA, Canada, Australia, Japa

Cover: Foto ©ninafisch / pixelio.de

Manufactured and distributed by brebook publishing software (www.brebook.com)

Eleanor Cecilia Donnelly

Out of Sweet Solitude

BY

ELEANOR C. DONNELLY.

"It is a fearful stake the poet casts,
When he comes forth from his sweet solitude
Of hopes, and songs, and visionary things,
To ask the iron verdict of the world."
MISS LANDON.

PHILADELPHIA:
J. B. LIPPINCOTT & CO.
1873.

Entered, according to Act of Congress, in the year 1873, by
J. B. LIPPINCOTT & CO.,
In the Office of the Librarian of Congress at Washington.

LIPPINCOTT'S PRESS,
PHILADELPHIA.

TO THE

RIGHT REVEREND JAMES FREDERIC WOOD,
BISHOP OF PHILADELPHIA.

THESE PAGES ARE, BY KIND PERMISSION,

INSCRIBED,

WITH THE RESPECTFUL REGARDS OF

THE AUTHORESS.

PREFACE.

The audacity of a comparatively unknown author who perpetrates the folly of a first book must needs find extenuation in a preface.

Apologies for obscure muses are so many and so tedious, that the writer of this book would despair of securing a patient perusal of either her preface or her poems did she not remember that a number of the latter have already drifted into print, and successively enjoyed a certain degree of popularity in religious journals and periodicals.

Encouraging as such favorable notice must indubitably be to an aspiring author, one who is not quite blinded with self-conceit cannot but see the risk of bearing the whole weight of authorship upon such slender supports. The lavish praise of personal friends is no greater guarantee of success with the critical public at large than is a mere local popularity sure to soften the "iron verdict of the world."

More than once, in thoughtful visits to public and private libraries, the writer has reverentially drawn from dim corner-recesses, or emancipated from the secret slavery of upper shelves, many a neglected book, both good and precious. Even if their dusty covers told no tale, the uncut pages were sufficient evidence of the oblivion to which they had been consigned.

Busy teeming brains had once, with fear and gladness, furnished forth this feast. Eager faces, throbbing hearts, and careful hands were all alive to greet and serve the invited guests. Every phrase was weighed and daintily prepared—every false quantity tested in the laboratory of æsthetic thought,—yet the contents of these dusty books were now, at last, less known to the living literary world outside the library walls, less valued by its critics, than might be the characters on a Chinese manuscript, or the hieroglyphs on an obscure Egyptian tomb.

To a new aspirant for literary success these mute preachers delivered a most trenchant sermon. In the studious silence the writer was haunted by a legion of mournful ghosts, whose pathetic lips had ever the same monotonous note of warning: "Yesterday for me; to-day for thee." And pondering on the many beautiful hopes that once had gilded each neglected volume, and considering the many fair thoughts pressed, like faded but still fragrant blossoms, between their unread pages, an earnest mind might well hesitate to make a venture fraught with such apparent failure to other and wiser pens.

But as every flower, no matter how humble, created with a divine purpose, fulfils the end of its creation by simply blooming in a grassy corner; as every bird, even if it be not a nightingale, is blessed in pouring its homely song into the grand chorus ascending ever to the Giver of all gifts: so may the simplest soul-flowers, so may the smallest heart-birds, brighten some quiet corners with their bloom and fill them full of melody.

And if, in Christian homes, these little poems distract for a space but one tired heart from its pressing personal sorrows,—if they gladden but a few earnest souls with the graceful accomplishment of a divine decree,—then may the writer

> "—— hope, as no unwelcome guest,
> At *the* warm fireside, when the lamps are lighted,
> To have *a* place reserved among the rest,
> Nor stand as one unsought and uninvited."

PHILADELPHIA, May 15, 1873.

CONTENTS.

SACRED LEGENDS.

	PAGE
Vision of the Monk Gabriel	11
Legend of the Robes	14
The Two Quests of the Abbot Paphnucius	17
The Bronze Berenice	23
Borgia's Vow	28
The Lily and the Palm	32
The Golden Psalm	34
Gualberto's Victory	36

POEMS OF THE CIVIL WAR

Missing	41
More Nurses	42
The Old Surgeon's Story	45
Rachel in the North	49
'Sixty-Four and 'Sixty-Five	50
Zum Jenseits	54
The Lady President's Ball	56
When the Great Rebellion's Over	58

MISCELLANEOUS POEMS.

The Sleeper's Sail	63
Unseen Yet Seen	66

CONTENTS.

	PAGE
Lost Lewie	69
A Red-Letter Day	72
In the Vintage	73
The Skeleton at the Feast	75
"Hic Jacet"	77
Song of the Snow-Bird	78
Mother's Corner	80
The Twilight Fairy	81
Called and Chosen	83
The Poet's Little Rival	85
Misunderstandings	86
Passing Footsteps	88
The Queen's Epitaph	90
Frank, my Darling	92
Fiat Voluntas Dei	94
Light in Darkness	94
Saint Martin's Summer	96
The Fate of the Fairy Swan	98
Feast of the Presentation	100
In Memoriam—Rev. Felix Joseph Barbelin	103

SACRED LEGENDS.

VISION OF THE MONK GABRIEL.

'Tis the soft twilight. Round the shining fender,
  Two at my feet and one upon my knee,
Dreamy-eyed Elsie, bright-lipped Isabel,
And thou, my golden-headed Raphael,
  My fairy, small and slender,
    Listen to what befell
    Monk Gabriel,
In the old ages ripe with mystery,—
Listen, my darlings, to the legend tender.

A bearded man, with grave but gentle look,
  His silence sweet with sounds
  With which the simple-hearted spring abounds:
  Lowing of cattle from the abbey grounds,
Chirping of insect and the building rook,
  Mingled like murmurs of a dreaming shell;
Quaint tracery of bird and branch and brook
Flitting across the pages of his book,
Until the very words a freshness took,—
    Deep in his cell
    Sate the monk Gabriel.

    In his book he read
  The words the Master to His dear ones said:
    "A little while and ye
      Shall see,
    Shall gaze on Me;
    A little while again
    Ye shall not see Me then."

VISION OF THE MONK GABRIEL.

"*A little while!*"
The monk looked up, a smile
Making his visage brilliant, liquid-eyed:
"O Thou, who gracious art
Unto the poor of heart,
O blessèd Christ!" he cried,
"Great is the misery
Of mine iniquity;
But would *I* now might see,
Might feast on Thee!"
The blood, with sudden start,
Nigh rent his veins apart—
(O condescension of the Crucified!)
In all the brilliancy
Of His humanity
The Christ stood by his side!

Pure as the early lily was His skin;
His cheek outblushed the rose,
His lips, the glows
Of autumn sunset on eternal snows.
And His deep eyes within
Such nameless beauties, wondrous glories, dwelt,
The monk in speechless adoration knelt.

In each fair hand, in each fair foot, there shone
The peerless stars He took from Calvary:
Around His brows in tenderest lucency
The thorn-marks lingered, like the flush of dawn;
And from the opening in His side there rilled
A light, so dazzling that the room was filled
With heaven; and, transfigured in his place,—
His very breathing stilled,—
The friar held his robe before his face,
And heard the angels singing!
'Twas but a moment; then, upon the spell

Of that sweet Presence, lo, a something broke:
A something, trembling, in the belfry woke,
   A shower of metal music flinging
O'er wold and moat, o'er park and lake and fell;
And, through the open window of the cell,
   In silver chimes came ringing.

      It was the bell
      Calling Monk Gabriel
Unto his daily task,
   To feed the paupers at the abbey gate.
No respite did he ask,
   Nor for a second summons idly wait;
But rose up, saying, in his humble way:
     "Fain would I stay,
     O Lord! and feast alway
   Upon the honeyed sweetness of Thy beauty.
But 'tis *Thy* will, not mine, I must obey;
   Help me to do my duty!"
The while the vision smiled,
The monk went forth, light-hearted as a child.

An hour thence, his duty nobly done,
  Back to his cell he came.
Unasked, unsought, lo, his reward was won!
   Rafters and walls and floor were yet aflame
With all the matchless glory of that Sun,
And in the centre stood the Blessèd One,
   (Praised be His holy name!)
Who for our sakes our crosses made His own
   And bore our weight of shame!

    Down on the threshold fell
    Monk Gabriel,
His forehead pressed upon the floor of clay;
And, while in deep humility he lay,
Tears raining from his happy eyes away,

"Whence is this favor, Lord?" he strove to say.
  The Vision only said,
  Lifting Its shining head:
"If thou hadst stayed, O son, *I* must have fled!"
MARCH, 1863.

LEGEND OF THE ROBES.

ELIZABETH, (by God's dear grace the spouse
Of Louis of Thuringia,) sat one day
In the fair quiet of her latticed room,
With Ysentrude—of all her maids best loved—
To bear her company.
                    The pure spring light
Crept through the ancient casement, and illumed
The noble beauty of the lady's face,
The chaste decorum of her simple robe,
Scarce richer than the beggar's russet cloak,
On which, with persevering love, she wrought;
Singing the while, with summer in her voice,
Sweet snatches of an old Hungarian hymn,
To which maid Ysentrude held meek refrain,
With sweeping lashes and low-drooping veil.
A step pulsed through the hall,—a manly step,—
And, in the doorway, framed (a picture fair),
Duke Louis stood, and smiled upon his spouse,
A tender smile, yet troubled.
                        Up she rose,
The fond Elizabeth, and coming, basked
In the mild lustre of his anxious eye;
The Christ-like pity on her girlish lip
Melting and mixing in her smile of joy;
While throbbing heart sent up its purest rose

To tremble through the olive of her cheek,
And bid him welcome there.
                    " What ill has chanced,
Dear love, to thee or thine, that this calm face
So sad a mask should wear?" the lady asked.
    " O spouse Elizabeth! we are undone!
Four envoys from thy father's court, below,
Come to crave audience with thy gentle self,
Who must respect their plea. What wilt thou do?
Thy love of God, and of His precious poor,
Has so inflamed thy generous soul with zeal,
That gems and silken robes are quite forsworn,
And all the pomp of ducal dignity
Sunk in obscure retreat. *I* do not chide
Thee, love, fair-blushing, like the morning sky!
Thy rosy charms, to *me*, can deck thee out
In raiment comelier than a queen's attire.
But if thou givest audience to these men,
Clad, as thou art, in this poor woollen robe,
They, knowing not the motive of thy deeds,
(That charity which gives, forgetting self,)
Will straightway swell with scandal and depart,
Burning to bruit what gossips burn to hear,
That Louis of Thuringia keeps his bride
In robes no better than a peasant dame's!"
  .With ear attentive to his tender words,
With kindling eye uplifted to his own,
Elizabeth was mute; but now her hand
Fell lightly as a snow-flake on his arm,
And through the silence came her silver voice:
    " Fret not thy soul, my Louis, with these cares,
But trust in God. Our noble guests are worn
And weary with long travel; do thou go
And bid them welcome to Thuringia's halls
Most generous. And when the feast is spread,
I shall attend you there!"

                    Her glorious smile,
Her pure uplifted brow, o'erawed him,
And he went away communing with her words.
—Then knelt the Lady 'Lisa where she stood,
Her little hands enclasped, her holy face
Brilliant with some strange lustre, as she prayed:
"O Lord! my Crucified! for Thy pure love
I have despoiled myself of royal robes,
And put away the vanity of gems!
Listen, O Best Belovèd! in Thy strength,
(Pure as the fleece and generous as the light!)
Behold me in my poverty and need,
And make me pleasing in mine husband's eyes!"
    Circled with veilèd maidens, down she went,
Transfigured with the passion of her prayer;
Her soft, slow step is herald to her coming,
And silence chains the lords who grace the feast.
    What 'mazement leaps to light their sluggish eyes,
What wonder parts their heavy-bearded lips!
While Louis folds his arms upon his chest,
Lifts his proud head, and smiles upon his bride.
    Her robe of silken sheen flowed o'er her feet
Sweeping the marble floor in waves of light;
Clasped at her throat, the yielding mantle sprung
To flood her graceful shoulders with its folds
Of velvet, azure as a summer's sky.
And, from her head (confined with diamond pins
Which lit her locks as stars the midnight gloom),
A fleecy veil fell, shimmering like spray,
Over her blushing cheeks, her pure, clear eyes!
"Sweet wife!" Duke Louis said, the while her hand
Lay, like a pearl, within his manly palm:
"Sweet wife!" ('twas but a whisper, yet she heard,)
"Thy face, methinks, doth sparkle like the sun,
And thy rich raiment———?"

Lady 'Lisa bowed
Her forehead, like a lily touched with sleep,
And while the color varied in her cheeks,
"Great is our God," she said, "and wondrous are His ways!"

THE TWO QUESTS OF THE ABBOT PAPHNUCIUS.

"Doth he not leave the ninety-nine in the desert, and go after that which was lost until he find it?"—ST. LUKE xv. 4.

THAIS, the sinner, beautiful and bold,
Clad in soft garments glittering with gold:
Her naked arms and throat with jewels bound,
Her splendid head with vines and tendrils crowned,
Once, in the heyday of her pride and passion,
Lay on her couch in oriental fashion,
And, lifting high a goblet gemmed with light,
(Dripping with wine, like amber melting bright,)
Full-throated, sang a nameless, shameless song,
Which even the echoes trembled to prolong.

A hundred courtiers round her couch reclined,
And slaves, like dusky shadows, moved behind;
While through the hall, to sounds of citherns rare,
The sparkling fountains cast into the air
Their scented waters (mirrors, showing clear
The silver lamps that glistened far and near):
And statues, ranged in many a polished row,
Caught from the rosy walls a kindred glow.

"A stranger craveth speech with Lady Thais,"—
It was a slave who spoke before the dais,

Prostrate on hands and knees, until he thrust
His lips and forehead to the very dust.

"Command him enter,"—and again went pealing
Her wild *brindisi* to the vaulted ceiling;
But the slave stirred not. "Art thou deaf and dumb?
Who would with Thais speak must hither come,
Or go unheard. How now, my prince of slaves?"
"It is a private audience he craves."

Between her lips flashed out the radiant pearl:
"Ha! ha! it is an arbitrary churl!
Tell me, my lords, was e'er such boldness heard?
The fellow hath assurance, on my word.
Bid him begone forthwith, and ne'er——: yet stay!
We'll punish his conceit some other way."
And gathering up her robes with careless grace,
The smile still hovering upon her face,
She crossed the long apartment, like a fawn,
Parted the hanging curtains, and was gone.

That inner room seemed strangely dim and damp
   After the light and song and floating musk:
No lustre save a single pendent lamp,
   And marble statues glaring through the dusk.
The Lady Thais shuddered as she drew
Her mantle closer, and abruptly threw
Her glittering eyes upon the unknown face
Of him who 'waited her in that still place.

It was an aged man with visage brown,
   Whose snowy hair upon his shoulders flowed;
White, waving beard and white-fringed eyes cast down:
   While dust and moil from many a weary road

Still lingered on his bare unsandaled feet,
And on his pilgrim garments, poor but neat.

All this she saw,—but saw as in a dream,
For by the single lamp's inconstant gleam,
Drawn by a potent spell, the wondering Greek
Saw naught distinctly save that visage meek,
That strange mild face,—those tranquil eyes downcast,—
Which made her struggling heart beat wild and fast.

"Lead me, I pray,"—he spoke in gravest tone,—
"Unto some spot where we may be alone."
"Within these walls," she murmured, "there is not
Than this small room a more sequestered spot.
No one can see us here, save God——' she broke
The sentence off,—for, like an echo, woke
The stranger's voice (sharp, as of one who trod
Upon an asp): "*None sees us here save God?*
O child!" he groaned, his lifted eyes on fire
With faith and zeal, and something purer, higher,
Than wretched Thais, trembling and afraid,
Had ever seen in sculptured art portrayed,—
"O child! if thou didst weigh the words just spoken,
 If thou didst believe, all guilty as thou art,
 That God, the Omnipresent, sees thy heart,
Thy inmost veins with sorrow would be broken!"

As one quick flash of lightning might illume
The dusky horrors of a charnel-room,—
Rending the sheets and mildewed shrouds asunder
From ghastly carcasses decaying under;
So flashed God's grace on that perverted heart,
And sin's foul winding-sheets were rent apart,—
Revealing there such loathsome degradation,
That Thais shuddered at the revelation.

Never before at feet of mortal man
Had knelt the proud, triumphant courtesan;
Never had blush or tear made soft her cheek,
Save to allure some young and timid Greek.
—But now she hesitates: her heaving chest
Betrays the contest raging in her breast;
The first deep blush of shame, the first hot tear
Of true contrition, on her cheek appear;
And down she sinks, her burning face close hidden,
And tears in torrents streaming forth unbidden,
Till, like the veriest slave, her brow is thrust
In dumb humiliation to the dust.

"Arise!" Paphnucius said: "and put aside
These guilty gems, these hellish robes of pride;
And clad in sober garments, let us hence
Unto thy new-born life of penitence."
And so he cast the silken curtains back,
   And stepped into the moonlight, clear as day:
Till, Thais following, they trod the track,
   Which, like a tawny ribbon, wound away
   Into the prayerful desert, still and gray—
Where many a heart, as passionate as hers,
Had rested 'mid those quiet worshipers.
And there Paphnucius led her past a well,
Unto a little cave, a disused cell,
And bade her enter in, devoid of pride,
And pray and fast, and, thenceforth, there abide.
—But Thais said, (the lovely, contrite Greek,)
While the hot tears made furrows in her cheek:
"What prayer, O holy father! shall I make
Unto the God who suffered for my sake?"
"Daughter!" he cried, "take not *His* awful name
So readily upon thy lips of shame.
Strike thou thy breast, and o'er and o'er repeat
(Prostrate in soul and body at His feet),

With sighs and tears, continually say:
'*Miserere mei! qui plasmasti me!*'
'Have mercy on me, Thou who formedst me!'
Let *this* your life-long supplication be.
And may His pitying love, indeed, be shown
When Death and Judgment claim thee for their own."

So saying, having sealed the little door,
The Abbot went away, and came no more.
And Thais kneeling, with neglected hair,
Struck her poor breast, and sobbed, and made her prayer,
Morning and night, within the desert gray:
"*Miserere mei! qui plasmasti me!*"
And with the Lamb's pure blood, and with her tears,
Washed clean the garments of her guilty years.

Hundreds of times the desert sun uprose:
Hundreds of times it set amid the snows
Of distant sands that, stretching white and dim,
Met softly the horizon's rosy rim.
And, like a quiet spirit robed in white,
Full forty times the new moon walked the night,
Her patient lustre silvering the cells
Of desert-saints,—the palm-trees and the wells.

And then Paphnucius, growing old and weak,
(Etherealized with love, as one who nears
The Paradise of God,) began to seek
Some token of the fair, repentant Greek,
Left in the wilderness in bygone years
To eat the bread of penance moist with tears.

And in the nights when death was at his door,
   And in the hush of days fast running out

(Living in prayer his life and labors o'er
Visions of souls haunting him evermore),
   The thought of Thais wrung his heart with doubt;
Till, full of zeal, he longed to know from Heaven,
If she had persevered and been forgiven.

What so insatiate as a saint's desire?
Kindled of God, it wasteth like a fire,
And driveth all before it mightily.
Paphnucius yielded. Rising in the night,
Deep into the desert journeyed he:
Driven to speak with Father Anthony
(That aged saint, who, like a shining light,
Was set to cheer each struggling cenobite).
And, having reached the sacred monastery,—
   Christ's garden blooming in a lonesome land,—
Begged the saint's benison, and on that very
   Day besought the Abbot to command
His whole community to meet in prayer,
   That God would grant Paphnucius his demand,
And exorcise his one consuming care.

Three days and nights the brethren did remain
Constant in intercession,—but in vain.
Three days and nights before Our Blessèd Lord
The inmost passion of their hearts they poured,
Though in profoundest silence they adored.
For each dim figure, in its cowl and cloak,
Prayed mentally, but never moved or spoke:
Each in its stall, so ghostly,—one might deem
The whole a quiet, recollected dream.

But God, at length, inclining to their aid,
On the third night His wondrous power displayed:
And Brother Paul, the simplest hermit there,
Beheld a glorious vision in his prayer.

The heavens were opened, like great doors, o'erhead,—
    And there revealed, 'mid saints of every tribe,
Good Brother Paul beheld a royal bed,
    Whose nameless beauties he could ne'er describe,
Save that 'twas lily-white and strangely lit,
With four celestial virgins guarding it.

Then Brother Paul cried out in ecstasy :
"This bed must be for Father Anthony!"
But, sweet and penetrating, rose a voice
That made the marrow of his bones rejoice :
"Be it made known to all, good Paul, by thee,
This bed is not for Father Anthony,
But for the sinner Thais,"—and, forthwith,
The vision paled before him, like a myth.

Close at his side Paphnucius knelt, and heard,
With kindred ecstasy each blessèd word.
The tears streamed down his face, like quiet rain,
The joy within his breast was almost pain ;
And when the vision ended, he arose,
And went his way,—how glad, God only knows.

THE BRONZE BERENICE.

THERE stands a statue in the open square
    Of an old minster town (no matter where),
Fashioned of bronze, and with a bashful grace
Melting the blank-eyed yearning of the face,
    Into a smile as pensive as a prayer.—
A woman tall and lovely,—as she stands,
She gathers to her breast with both her hands

A little veil, whereon, divinely chaste,
The suffering visage of a Man is traced.
While round her slender feet a wealth of flowers
The marble base deliciously embowers;
And where the tallest grow, each, like a gem,
Blushing along her tunic's golden hem,
The eager hands of children day by day,
Rosy and reverent, pluck each dewy spray,
And in their aprons bear the blooms away.

Trembling tradition basking in the sun,
Gray-haired, but golden-mouthed, to every one
Who, unaccustomed, walks that quiet street,
The legend of the statue doth repeat:
A broken strain of music drifting down
The storied ages to that quaint old town.

"If I but touch His garment's hem," she said,
"I shall be healed;" and then her veilèd head
The kneeling Berenice in languor drooped
Low in the dust. Behind the Master stooped,
She pressed her pale lips on His tunic's hem.
One kiss—and lo! while all before her swam
(Her eyes star-dazzled, every power in play,
And every ache and ailment cast away),
With one electric flood of health and life,
And glorious strength, her bounding veins were rife!
"Who," spake a mellow Voice above her,—"who
Hath touched Me?" Piercing the vast crowd through,
A tongue made answer, "Lo! the people now
Throng Thee and press on Thee, O Lord! and Thou
Wouldst know who touched Thee?" Sweeter still and
      low,
The golden Voice: "I feel the virtue go
Forth from Me even now, therefore I know

By that same token, some one touches Me."
—Then Berenice crept forward tremblingly,
And with a worshipful and bashful trust,
Laid down her glowing forehead in the dust,
And whispered: " It was I, poor Berenice;"
And the Voice answered, rich and tremulous,
" Daughter, thy faith hath healed thee,—go in peace."

Slow-stepped and lingering, as Eve of yore
Went forth from Paradise; for evermore
   Turning to look upon that Face sublime,
Whose majesty the meanest might adore,
   Whose loveliness should haunt her through all time,
Went Berenice. The breathless multitude
(Thronging the way to where the Master stood;
Scaling the trees, and mounting, thick and fast,
Upon each other's shoulders) struggled past,
A living wall about Him; till, at last,
She saw His face no more; but onward sped,
Glad as a vision from the blessèd dead,
To the old castle near Jerusalem,
Where dwelt her brothers. There, alone with them,
She many months abode, and wrought and prayed,
And through the house a ceaseless sunshine made.
—But often in the night she rose and said,
" I am unworthy!" then beside her bed
Knelt with her hands before her eyes; and then
Leaned from her lattice at the dawn, again
Crying, " I am unworthy!" Through the mist,
Seeing but One; and from the amethyst
Of moonlit hollows hearing but one sound,—
The voice of Him who, pitiful, had crowned
Her life with healing.

              Then she secret wept,
And yearned to see Him once again; while leapt

A glory to her lips: "Would they might touch
Once more His sacred feet! Alas, for such
As me that boon were not. Poor Berenice!
Spake He not thus: 'My daughter, go in peace'?"

Haply the heart on which the canker preys
   May dull its pain with labor's anodyne,
And in the busy duties of the days
   Smother its sighs. But when the stars out shine,
And shadows fall, and all the household sleeps,
Grief walks the gloom, and wrings her hands, and weeps.

So, many a night, this woman battled strong,
   Tearful and passionate. At the dawn to rise,
   Smoothing her ruffled tresses from her eyes,
To hide her sorrow 'neath a spinning song,
And all the day, in work, her woe disguise.

Until there came an hour when the street,
Under her window, trembled 'neath the feet
Of many passers: curses, shouts, and screams
Waking the sluggish from their nooning dreams;
And all the rabble, all the brutal mob,
Of the great city swarming there.
                            A throb,
As if her heart had burst,—a deadly chill
   Freezing her blood,—and Berenice looks down
   Upon a pinioned Man who wears a crown
Of cruel thorns, whence many a bloody rill
   Runs down His pallid face; His shoulders bowed
   Under a mighty cross, and all the crowd
Goading Him forward with a desperate will.

Dream of her night, and Vision of her day!
Was He to come at last this dolorous way?
His face with tangled tresses, blood-besprent,
His flowing beard defiled, His garments rent;

The broad chest heaving 'neath the ponderous load,
And every step a blood-print on the road,—
Was He to come at last this dolorous way?

Crying no more, "I am unworthy!" lo!
She stretches forth her arms and murmurs slow:
"O Love! sweet Lord! my place is at Thy feet!"
And straightway slips into the angry street.

No gentle fellowship for such as she,—
   The oaths and clamors of the mob increase;
   But through the midst the Lady Berenice
Goeth unharmed; the brutal soldiery
Checking their Victim, as on bended knee
Before Him in the dust the lady bows,
   Pouring the fondest kisses on His feet,
   And piteous tears; the while her fingers fleet
Unbind the veil of linen from her brows.
A moonlight smile, pathetically sweet,
Out of His languid eyes is seen to shine,—
And reaching forth, the Sufferer divine
Receives the linen from her trembling hand
And puts it to His bleeding face; so grand
In all His sacred helplessness, that none
Dare lift a finger till the deed is done.

Then on the folded palms of Berenice,
With that same tender smile of wordless peace,
He lays it down. The crowd press shouting on;
And from her stupor, like a frighted fawn,
The lady wakes to see upon her veil,
In bloody print, the thorn-crowned head and pale
Of Him who to His cruel death has gone.

*   *   *   *   *   *   *   *   *

So far the legend. 'Neath the yearning face
Of the bronze Berenice the children swarm;

White glancing arms, and dimpled fingers warm
With sunshine, busy at the statue's base.
And when one (coming from new lands to see
The marvels of the old) asks, smilingly:
"Wherefore the tallest flowers always pull?
The tallest are not the most beautiful,"
The bright, shy faces of the children glow,
And through their fringy lashes, peering low:
"Because the flowers that touch her garment's hem
Have wondrous powers of healing lodged in them."
"And why?"   "Because—because" (and like to birds
Whose aimless speech hath but one groove of words)—
"Because they touch her garment's holy hem."

O shade of Berenice! fair, faithful ghost!
Haunting the crystal air of some old coast
Purely celestial, let the children go,
And thine own answer make.   The bronze lips blow
   Into a smile; in far-off accents calm,
From out the polished throat flow tranquilly
The liquid words: "*Non nobis, Domine,*
   Sed nomini tuo—da gloriam!"

BORGIA'S VOW.

In her royal mantle of gold and lace,
   In crown of diamonds and clasps of pearls,
With the long hair brushed from her lovely face,
   Engirdling her with massive curls,
The fair dead empress lay at rest,
Her hands crossed meekly on her breast;

The first sweet bride of Charles the Fifth,
   The young and blooming Isabelle,

In the prime of her beauty and brilliant gifts,
    Cut off from the people she loved so well;
Through the length and breadth of sunny Spain
The tears of the mourners fell like rain.

And out from the chapel at dear Madrid,
    Where the tapers burned and the censers swung,
Where flowers were strewn on the coffin lid,
    And the solemn mass by the bishops sung,
Forth to Granada, fair and old,
The funeral train, like a torrent, rolled

How fresh the breath of the morning came
    From the orange gardens, left and right!
The sunshine tipped each lance with flame,
    And bathed the banners in amber light;
And the little birds sang clear and strong,
As the solemn cortége swept along.

Close to the bier, with bended head,
    Francis, the Duke of Gandia, rode;
Sorrow and love for the queenly dead
    Crushing his heart with a leaden load:
While his spouse, the Duchess Eleanor,
In a stately litter went before.

Well might the Duke look pale and sad,
    Well might the tears of the Duchess fall;
For the noblest friend they ever had
    Lay slumbering 'neath that velvet pall;
And never again might court or throne
The magic spell of her presence own.

Lost to the world that matchless face,
    With its radiant eyes and floating hair;
That form replete with royal grace,
    Those hands, like lilies, small and fair;

BORGIA'S VOW.

That blush, that smile, that silver voice,
Whose song made king and court rejoice.

Past like a dream those hours of peace
   They spent in chapel at her side;
Or roaming 'mid the orange-trees,
   In palace-gardens, cool and wide;
Her dark eye kindling like a star
When Francis touched the sweet guitar.

Remembering, though an empress, she
   Won ever, by her virtues pure,
The homage due her dignity
   From wise and simple, rich and poor;
Well might her subjects' tears o'erflow
When Death their royal rose laid low!

And while they mourned, and while they wept,
   The weary hours of marching sped,
And into old Granada swept
   The long procession of the dead;
Duke Francis riding still the first,
In melancholy thought immersed.

And then the ancient streets were stirred
   With the rushing sound of many feet;
And over it all the monks were heard
   Singing their anthem slow and sweet;
While the trumpets blared, and high and low
The bells tolled sadly to and fro;

Tolled sadly east, tolled sadly west,
   As on to the royal vaults they went;
Each head uncovered to that guest,
   And every knee in homage bent,
Responsive, while in one grand prayer,
The *De Profundis* rent the air.

BORGIA'S VOW.

Then in the chant and solemn rites
    There comes a sudden hush and halt;
The Borgia and his brother knights
    Approach the entrance of the vault;
And, falling on one knee, prepare
Upon their sabre-hilts to swear
Their sovereign's corpse lies truly there.

Back rolled the ponderous coffin-lid;
    O Heaven! hide that hideous sight!
The pride and glory of Madrid,
    Darling of king, and court's delight,
There in the shuddering sunshine lay
A sickening mass of foul decay!

From lip and eye the worms escaped,
    And, crawling, fed on cheek and nose
    (Which, erst as pure as mountain snows,
Were now with black corruption craped);
While from the livid, loathsome shape
    So terrible a stench arose,
That right and left the courtiers fled,
And left Duke Francis with the dead.

He did not turn, he did not flee,
    Although his very blood ran cold,
    And nature trembled to behold
Amid that wreck the mockery
    Of flashing gems and cloth of gold;
But, by the light of *that* lost star,
He saw how frail earth's glories are.

Still on his knees beside the bier,
    He cried: "O peerless Isabelle!
O sovereign lady, fair and dear!
    What means this monstrous spectacle?

Can this most foul corruption be
All that is left, my queen, of thee?"

Then with uplifted arms: "Great Lord!
    Look down upon Thy creature lonely,
As on the cross-hilt of his sword
    He swears to love and serve Thee only;
Far from the world, henceforth, to hide
In the wounded heart of the Crucified!

" O sovereign Beauty! at whose breath
    The bonds of flesh are rent and riven;
Who knowest not decay or death
    Within Thy fair immortal heaven:
Henceforth, O Master! King divine!
My life, my love, my all are Thine!"

  * * * * * *

High at the footstool of the Lord,
    Wide open lay the Book of Life,—
And there, while white-robed saints adored,
    And all the air with song was rife,
A seraph with a pen of flame
Inscribed Saint Francis Borgia's name.

THE LILY AND THE PALM.

"Stay! whither goest thou?"—a hand was laid
Upon the shoulder of a veilèd maid,
    Speeding at sunrise through the Roman streets:
And at the gate Cassandra,—jewel-starred
His uniform,—a soldier of the Guard
    (One of those mighty, merciless athletes,

Known as Maximian's Guard Imperial,
Who studded, statue-like, the brazen wall)
Stepped from the shadow, stern and bronzed of face,
And held the virgin in that silent place.

'Twas in the evil days of pagan wrath,
While yet Dulcitius mowed the aftermath
Of stainless victims, eager for the crown,
Professing Christ before the howling town,
And for Him laying life and freedom down.
When, torn from torch-lit cell and chapel dim
(Their lips yet throbbing with the Latin hymn),
Soldier, civilian, virgin, widow, priest,
Met at the rack, as at a marriage-feast.

"Stay! whither goest thou?" The gentle girl,—
Anysia by name,—a very pearl
Of sanctity and loveliness,—her veil
Drew closer round her features, pure and pale;
And while the cruel hand upon her arm
Tightened its grasp, and filled her with alarm,
She made the sacred sign upon her brow,
But spake no word.
            "How now, my pretty, how?"
The soldier laughed; "thy form is full of grace:
Lift up thy veil, and let me see thy face.
Who art? and whither goest thou?"

Anysia spoke; the accents seemed to drip,
Like golden globules, from her virgin lip:
"Behold a servant poor of Christ the Lord!
Unto His dear assembly do I go."
"Not so," the soldier roughly sneered,—"not so;
I'll fetch thee to *our* rites, and, by my sword!
To-day, O maid! thou'lt sacrifice to Pan,
And not thy Christ!"

So saying, he began
To tear the wimple from her pallid face,
And shame the virgin in that public place.
—Quick rose the vivid blushes to her brow,
And clasping on her breast her hands of snow,
From side to side, a frightened fawn and faint,
She sent her timid wail of sad complaint.

Mad with desire, to which resistance lent
An added fire, the Roman soldier bent
Upon his prey a glare of angry guilt,
And laid his hand upon his sabre-hilt:
"Shriek till thou faintest! weep till thine eyes run dry!
None heed thy tears, my sweet, nor hear thy cry;
Even thy Christ is deaf as all the rest."
And so he plunged his sword into her breast.
Poor broken flower! all trembling, down she drooped,
The lily veil from off her temples looped,
Dyed with her virgin blood to rosy red:
And her meek, glazing eye, like harebell, hid
Under the shadow of the long-lashed lid.
"Dead—and most beautiful!" the soldier said,
Stooping above her,—"thou wert true, my steel."
And then, with folded arms, turned on his heel,
Never to meet again those tender eyes
Till saint and sinner at the Judgment rise.

THE GOLDEN PSALM.

'Tis written of the Roman wife, Saint Frances,
   Kneeling at vespers in her oratory,
(The sunshine piercing with its myriad lances
   The dusky windows till they glowed with glory,)

That, as the light
  Fell on the pages of her missal white,
And she began the psalm, "*Beatus vir*,"
Down the long corridor, resounding clear
And mellow as the warble of a bird,
  Her husband's voice she heard,
Calling her to fulfill some household duty.

  Leaving the prayer unread,
  The psalm unsaid,
Saint Frances rose in all her wifely beauty,
  And joined De Pontians: and bowed her head
Upon his shoulder with a trustful smile.
  Brought at his bidding wine and wheaten bread,
And while he ate, most tenderly the while
  His weary thoughts to pleasant channels led.

  Then back she bloomed
Into the dim old chapel, and resumed
Her broken prayer. But at " *Beatus vir*,"
Again her husband's voice rose sharp and clear,
Clipping, as with a sword, her soaring wings,
To bring her, trembling, down to mundane things.

  Once more, her book
Leaving upon her *prie-dieu*, all unheeded,
The fair young wife no second summons needed,
  Nor showed unwillingness in word or look;
But, with angelic patience, took the skein
  Of tangled duties from her spouse's hand,
And, smiling, wove them silken-smooth again
  Upon the precious reels of self-command.

  The sweet task done,
  And on her bended knees once more begun

The interrupted psalm (O bliss untold !)—
Upon the sacred page beneath her eyes,
Sparkling and glowing with the sweet surprise,
 "BEATUS VIR" *was writ in lines of gold!*

GUALBERTO'S VICTORY.

A MOUNTAIN pass so narrow that a man
Riding that way to Florence, stooping, can
Touch with his hand the rocks on either side,
And pluck the flowers that in the crannies hide.
 Here, on Good Friday, centuries ago,
Mounted and armed, John Gualbert met his foe:
Mounted and armed as well, but riding down
To the fair city from the woodland brown,
This way and that, swinging his jeweled whip,
A gay old love-song on his careless lip,
And on his charger's neck the reins loose thrown.

 An accidental meeting; but the sun
Burned on their brows, as if it had been one
Of deep design,—so deadly was the look
Of mutual hate their olive faces took;
As (knightly courtesy forgot in wrath),
Neither would yield his enemy the path.
 "Back!" cried Gualberto. "Never!" yelled his foe;
And on the instant, sword in hand, they throw
Them from their saddles, nothing loath,
And fall to fighting, with a smothered oath.
 A pair of shapely, stalwart cavaliers,
Well-matched in stature, weapons, weight, and years,

Theirs was a long, fierce struggle on the grass,
Thrusting and parrying up and down the pass;
Swaying from left to right, in combat clenched,
Till all the housings of their steeds were drenched
With brutal gore: and ugly blood-drops oozed
Upon the rocks, from head and hands contused.
But at the close, when Gualbert stopped to rest,
His heel was planted on his foeman's breast;
And looking up, the fallen courtier sees,
As in a dream, gray rocks and waving trees
Before his glazing vision faintly float,
While Gualbert's sabre glitters at his throat.

"Now die, base wretch!" the victor fiercely cries,
His heart of hate outflashing from his eyes:
"Never again, by the all-righteous Lord!
Shalt thou, with life, escape this trusty sword,—
Revenge is sweet!" And upward glanced the steel.
But ere it fell,—dear Lord! a silvery peal
Of voices chanting in the town below,
Grave, ghostly voices chanting far below,
Rose, like a fountain's spray from spires of snow,
And chimed and chimed to die in echoes slow.

In the sweet silence following the sound,
Gualberto and the man upon the ground
Glared at each other with bewildered eyes
(The glare of hunted deer on leashèd hound);
And then the vanquished, struggling to arise,
Made one last effort, while his face grew dark
With pleading agony: "Gualberto! hark!
The chant—the hour—thou know'st the olden fashion,—
The monks below intone our Lord's dear Passion.
Oh! by this cross!"—and here he caught the hilt
Of Gualbert's sword,—"and by the Blood once spilt

Upon it for us both long years ago,
Forgive—forget—and spare a fallen foe!"

The face that bent above grew white and set
(Christ or the demon?—in the balance hung):—
The lips were drawn,—the brow bedewed with sweat,—
But on the grass the harmless sword was flung:
And stooping down, the hero, generous, wrung
The outstretched hand. Then, lest he lose control
Of the but half-tamed passions of his soul,
Fled up the pathway, tearing casque and coat
To ease the tempest throbbing at his throat;
Fled up the crags, as if a fiend pursued,
And paused not till he reached a chapel rude.

There, in the cool dim stillness, on his knees,
Trembling, he flings himself, and, startled, sees
Set in the rock a crucifix antique,
From which the wounded Christ bends down to speak:
  "*Thou hast done well, Gualberto. For My sake
  Thou didst forgive thine enemy; now take
  My gracious pardon for thy times of sin,
  And from this day a better life begin.*"

White flashed the angels' wings above his head,
Rare, subtile perfumes through the place were shed;
And golden harps and sweetest voices poured
Their glorious hosannas to the Lord,
Who in that hour, and in that chapel quaint,
Changed by His power, by His dear love's constraint,
Gualbert the sinner into John the saint.

POEMS OF THE CIVIL WAR.
1861–1865.

"MISSING."

In the cool, sweet hush of a wooded nook,
    Where the May-buds sprinkle the green old ground,
And the wind, and the birds, and the limpid brook
    Murmur their dreams with a drowsy sound,—
Who lies so still in the plushy moss,
    With his pale cheek pressed to a breezy pillow,
Couched where the light and shadows cross
    Through the flickering fringe of the willow?
        Who lies, alas!
So still, so chill, in the whispering grass?

A soldier, clad in the zouave dress,
    A bright-haired man, with his lips apart,
One hand thrown up o'er his frank, dead face,
    And the other clutching his pulseless heart,
Lies there in the shadows cool and dim,
    His musket brushed by a trailing bough;
A careless grace in his quiet limbs,
    And a wound on his manly brow:
        A wound, alas!
Whose dark clots blood the pleasant grass.

The violets peer from their dusky beds
    With a tearful dew in their great pure eyes;
The lilies quiver their shining heads,
    Their pale lips full of a sad surprise;
And the lizard darts through the glistening fern,
    And the squirrel rustles the branches hoary;

Strange birds fly out, with a cry, to burn
  Their wings in the sunset glory,
    While the shadows pass
O'er the quiet face on the dewy grass.

God pity the bride who waits at home,
  With her lily cheeks and her violet eyes,
Dreaming the sweet old dream of love,
  While the lover is walking in paradise!
God strengthen her heart as the days go by,
  And the long, drear nights of her vigils follow;
Nor bird, nor moon, nor whispering wind
  May breathe the tale of the hollow!
    Alas! alas!
The secret is safe with the woodland grass.

MORE NURSES.

Fold away all your bright-tinted dresses,
  Turn the key on your jewels to-day,
And the wealth of your tendril-like tresses
  Braid back in a serious way.
No more delicate gloves, no more laces,
  No more trifling in boudoir or bower,
But come with your souls in your faces
  To meet the stern wants of the hour.

Look around! By the torchlight unsteady
  The dead and the dying seem one.
What? trembling and paling already,
  Before your dear mission's begun?
These wounds are more precious than ghastly
  Love presses her lip to each scar,

While she chants of that glory, so vastly
    Transcending the horrors of war.

Pause here by this bedside. How mellow
    The light showers down on that brow!
Such a brave, brawny visage! Poor fellow!
    Some homestead is missing him now.
Some wife shades her eyes in the clearing,
    Some mother sits moaning, distressed,
While the loved one lies faint, but unfearing,
    With the enemy's ball in his breast.

Here's another; a lad—a mere stripling—
    Picked up on the field almost dead,
The blood through his sunny hair rippling
    From a horrible gash in the head.
They say he was first in the action:
    Gay-hearted, quick-handed, and witty,
He fought till he dropped with exhaustion,
    At the gates of that far Southern city.

Fought and fell 'neath the guns of that city,
    With a spirit surpassing his years,—
Lift him up in your large-hearted pity,
    And wet his pale lips with your tears.
Touch him gently; most sacred the duty
    Of dressing that poor shattered hand.
God spare him to rise in his beauty,
    And battle once more for his land!

Who groaned? What a passionate murmur!
    "In Thy mercy, O God! let me die!"
Ha! surgeon, your hand must be firmer,
    That musket-ball's broken his thigh.
Turn the light on those poor furrowed features,
    Gray-haired and unknown? Bless thee, brother!

O Heaven! that one of Thy creatures
   Should e'er work such woe on another!

Wipe the sweat from his brow with your kerchief,
   Let the old tattered collar go wide;
See—he stretches out blindly to search if
   The surgeon still stands at his side.
"My son's over yonder—a rebel—
   'Twas—'twas *his* ball that entered my thigh!"
And again he bursts out, all atremble,
   "In Thy mercy, O God! let me die!"

Pass on: it is useless to linger,
   While others are claiming your care;
There is need for your delicate finger,
   For your womanly sympathy, there.
There are sick ones athirst for caressing,
   There are dying ones raving of home:
There are wounds to bind up with a blessing,
   And shrouds to make ready for some.

They have gathered about you the harvest
   Of death in its ghastliest view;
The nearest as well as the farthest,
   The traitor as well as the true.
And crowned with your beautiful patience,
   Made sunny with love at the heart,
You must balsam the wounds of a nation,
   Nor falter, nor shrink from your part.

Up and down through the wards where the fever
   Stalks noisome and gaunt and impure,
You must go with your steadfast endeavor
   To comfort, to counsel, to cure.
I grant you the task's superhuman,
   But strength will be given to you

To do for these dear ones what woman
    Alone, in her pity, can do.

And the lips of the mothers will bless you,
    Our angels, sweet-visaged and pale!
And the little ones run to caress you,
    And the wives and the sisters cry "Hail!"
And e'en if you drop down unheeded,
    What matter? God's ways are the best,—
You have poured out your life where 'twas needed,
    And *He* will take care of the rest.

THE OLD SURGEON'S STORY.

'TWAS in a Southern hospital, a month ago or more,
(God save us! how the days drag on these weary times of
    war!)
They brought me, in the sultry noon, a youth whom they
    had found
Deserted by his regiment upon the battle-ground,
And bleeding his young life away through many a gaping
    wound.

Dark-haired and slender as a girl, a handsome lad was he,
Despite the pallor of his wounds, each one an agony.
A ball had carried off his arm, and zigzag passage frayed
Into his chest; so wild a rent, that, when it was displayed,
I, veteran surgeon that I was, turned white as any maid.

"There is no hope?" he slowly said, noting my changing
    cheek;
I only shook my head; I dared not trust myself to speak.

But in that wordless negative the boy had read his doom,
And turned about, as best he could, and lay in silent gloom,
Watching the summer sunlight make a glory of the room.

"My little hero!" said a voice, and then a woman's hand
Lay, like a lily, on his curls: "God grant you self-command!"
"Mother!"—how full that thrilling word of pity and alarm!—
"You here? my sweetest mother here?" And with his one poor arm
He got about her neck, and drew her down with kisses warm.

"All the long sultry night, when out" (he shuddered as he said)
"On yonder field I lay among the festering heaps of dead,
With awful faces close to mine, and clots of bloody hair,
And dead eyes gleaming through the dusk with such a rigid stare:
Through all my pain, O mother mine, I only prayed one prayer.

"Through all my pain (and ne'er I knew what suffering was before)
I only prayed to see your face, to hear your voice, once more;
The cold moon shone into my eyes,—my prayer seemed all in vain."
"My poor deluded boy!" she sobbed; her mother-fount of pain
O'erflowing down her darkening cheeks in drops like thunder-rain.

"Accursed be he whose cruel hand has wrought my son such ill!"
The boy sprang upright at the word, and shrieked aloud, "Be still!

You know not what you say. O God! how shall I tell the
   tale!
How shall I smite her as she stands!" And with a moaning
   wail
He prone among the pillows dropped, his visage ashen
   pale.

"It was a bloody field," he said, at last, like one who
   dozed;
"I know not how the day began; I know not how it
   closed.
I only know we fought like fiends, begrimed with blood
   and dust,
And did our duty to a man, as every soldier must,
And gave the rebels ball for ball, and paid them thrust for
   thrust.

"But when our gallant general rode up and down the line,
The sunlight striking on his sword until it flashed like wine,
And cried aloud (God rest his soul!) with such a cheery
   laugh:
'Charge bayonets, boys! Pitch into them, and scatter them
   like chaff!'
One-half our men were drunk with blood, and mad the
   other half.

"My veins ran fire. O Heaven! hide the horrors of that
   plain!
We charged upon the rebel ranks and cut them down like
   grain.
One fair-haired man ran on my steel,—I pierced him
   through and through;
The blood upspirted from his wound and sprinkled me like
   dew.
'Twas strange, but as I looked, I thought of Cain and him
   he slew.

"Some impulse moved me to kneel down and touch him where he fell;
I turn'd him o'er,—I saw his face,—the sight was worse than hell!
There lay my brother—curse me not!—pierced by *my* bayonet!"
—O Christ! the pathos of that cry I never shall forget,—
Men turned away to hide their tears, for every eye was wet.

And the hard-featured woman-nurse, a sturdy wench was she,
Dropped down among us in a swoon, from very sympathy.
—"I saw his face, the same dear face which once (would we had died
In those old days of innocence!) was ever by my side,
At board or bed, at book or game, so fresh and merry-eyed.

"And now to see it white and set,—to know the deed was mine!
A madness seized me as I knelt, accursed in God's sunshine.
I did not heed the balls which fell around us thick as rain,
I did not know my arm was gone; I felt nor wound nor pain:
I only stooped and kissed those lips which ne'er would speak again.

"'Oh, Louis!' (and the lad looked up, and brushed a tear aside)—
"'Oh, Louis! brother of my soul! my boyhood's fearless guide!
By the bright heaven where thou stand'st,—by thy big-hearted faith,—
By these the tears our mother sheds,—by this, my failing breath,—
Forgive me for that murderous thrust that wounded thee to death.

"Forgive me! I would yield my life, to give thee thine, my
    brother!
What's this?—Don't shut the sunlight out; I cannot see
    my mother!
The air blows sweet from yonder field! Dear Lou, put
    up your sword.
Let's weave a little daisy-chain upon this pleasant
    sward——"
And with a smile upon his mouth, the boy slept in the
    Lord.

RACHEL IN THE NORTH.

My boy—my pride—my strong-limbed Absalom!
    Dead! dead? Who dared to whisper "*dead*" of thee?
Dead on the field,—thy bright locks stained with loam,
    A bullet in thy breast,—sword-gashes three.

It cannot be. Oh, friends! it must not be!
    My only son,—the nursling of my breast,—
The blue-eyed boy who sat upon my knee,
    And in my mother-arms took cradled rest;

Was there no other heart to flesh their steel?
    No other blood to slake their cruel thirst?
Is there no virtue in the wild appeal
    Of stricken hearts? O God! my brain will burst!

"Keep thee good cheer, my mother" (last he wrote),
    "This strife soon o'er,—I'll soon return to thee!"
Return? Brave boy! thy tender words have smote
    My stony heart, and tears gush ceaselessly.

Return? Ah, woe! the merry troops may go,
   And blue-eyed boys may march to fife and drum:
Bayonets may flash and starry banners flow,
   My blue-eyed boy will never go or come.

Mothers may lean from casements to behold
   Their bright-haired sons come marching to the door;
Caps will be doffed, brows lifted as of old,
   My bright-haired son will never greet me more!

Out on the cruel field he lies, dear God!
   Whom three nights gone I pillowed safe and warm,
Thinking the down scarce soft enough,—the sod,
   Alas! the bloody sod now beds his form.

I watch—I watch—I cannot realize
   The bitter truth; but door and window watch:
His well-known eyes to see 'mid passing eyes,
   His well-known hand upon the garden-latch.

I watch—I wait. I had such hopes and schemes
   Of what might be if he were home once more.
Fame! glory! perish—empty, hollow dreams!
   My glory's dead. And this, O Heaven, is war!

'SIXTY-FOUR AND 'SIXTY-FIVE.

I.

Come to the crowning of the King,
   The gracious heir of Time,
While cannons roar, and pæans ring,
   And merry joybells chime;
While cares take wing, and everything
   To pleasure seems alive,
Come to the crowning of the King,
   The glorious 'Sixty-Five!

II.

Last night we stirred the blazing fire,
  When the midnight-hour was striking,
And bade them fill our glasses higher
  With liquor to our liking;
And while we drank those toasts once more,
  Which such sweet hours revive,
We closed the door on 'Sixty-Four
  And welcomed 'Sixty-Five.

III.

We did not shout when we hurried out
  The Old Year, gaunt and hoary:
For we honored him for what had been,
  And loved him for his glory.
And we thought of pleasures at an end,
  And joys that come no more,
And we cried, "God rest our honest friend,
  Departed 'Sixty-Four!"

IV.

And then we heard the sweet bells ring,
  The wedding-bells Elysian,
And saw the fair brides of the year
  Sweep past us, like a vision;
And then a troop of rosy elves
  Skipped lightly o'er the floor,
The babes of benediction born
  In happy 'Sixty-Four.

V.

But, then, alas! alas! alas!
  We heard the roar of battle,
And saw, as in a burnished glass,
  Brave men, like slaughtered cattle,—

Wounded and maimed with shot and shell,
    And weltering in their gore,
Our true, our gallant boys who fell
    In hapless 'Sixty-Four!

VI.

Oh! we pillow our dying darlings well,
    And we damp their shrouds with tears,
From the child in its spotless innocence
    To the grandsire full of years;
But down on the Southern battle-plain
    Who pillows the sick and sore?
And who weeps over the nameless slain
    That fell in 'Sixty-Four?

VII.

Though the door is closed on that old, old year,
    And its face shut out forever,
With its babes and its brides and its slaughtered dead,
    Shut out—shut out forever!
Yet the hopes and joys which died in the Old,
    In the New Year may revive,
And the hearts that were wounded in 'Sixty-Four
    May be healed in 'Sixty-Five.

VIII.

Though we cannot call up from the churchyard snows
    The treasures they hold securely;
Though our hearts are sick for the smile of those
    Who sleep in the Lord,—yet surely,
As out of the cactus, rough with thorns,
    A rich bright flower may thrive,
The griefs which were briers in 'Sixty-Four
    May be blossoms in 'Sixty-Five.

IX.

If fathers, brothers, husbands, sons,
   'Neath the flag they loved enlisted,
Have dropped in the blaze of the roaring guns,
   And perished, unassisted ;
Though homes be drear, and hearts be sore,
   To do God's will we strive ;
And the dear ones slaughtered in 'Sixty-Four
   Are the martyrs of 'Sixty-Five !

X.

Then, brothers, a health to the year that's gone,
   And a health to the year to be ;
The young King mounts the vacant throne
   With a smile of victory.
War at his feet, expiring, lies
   While the clouds melt in the South :
And the dove sails up the sunny skies
   With the olive in her mouth.

XI.

And the dumb have speech, and eyes, once dim,
   Now clearly, brightly see ;
And the fetters fall from many a limb,
   That ne'er before was free.
And voices arise from swamp and shore,
   Like the hum of bees in the hive,
From those who were slaves in 'Sixty-Four,
   The freemen of 'Sixty-Five !

XII.

Then come to the crowning of the King,
   The monarch of grace and glory,
Whose golden fame the bards shall sing,
   Whose name shall be writ in story.

And bless the Lord we all adore,
   Through whom we live and thrive,
And pray that the awful scourge of war,
The vices and wrongs of 'Sixty-Four,
May die with its dead, and rise no more,
   To haunt us in 'Sixty-Five!

ZUM JENSEITS.

Who calls through the solemn silence,—
   Tenderly calls my name?
Whose eyes, through the dusky gloom of night,
   Waken me with their flame?
Whose tranquil kiss, on my burning brow,
Trembles and melts like early snow?

Thou hast the voice of my mother,
   Thou hast her fair dead mouth;
Thou hast the eyes of my brother brave,
   Who fell last year in the South;
And the flowing hair and the classic head
Of my sweet young sister, long since fled.

Oh, the weary years of sorrow!
   Oh, the months and weeks forsaken!
Oh, the days and nights of pain I've known
   Since those I loved were taken!
(Draw near to me, thou silent Guest,
And lay my head upon thy breast.)

While others frolicked with roses,
   I only found the thorns,—
The flowers slipped through my fingers,
   And only left the thorns;

ZUM JENSEITS.

If blessed is he who suffers, Lord!
   And blessed is he who mourns,
Then doubly blessed am I, for strife
And woe have eaten up my life.

I am weary, very weary,
   Yet methinks that I could rest,
If but this tender Angel hold
   My cheek upon his breast.
What's this? Dissolved,—ye walls of clay?
My chains and fetters drop away!

I know thee now, thou Spirit!
   O Death! I know thee well.
Good Death! sweet Death! whose voice to me
   Is like a wedding-bell;
Since thou hast kissed my faded cheek,
A bonnier bridegroom I'll not seek.

Thy loving arms embrace me,
   Thy deep eyes swim with light;
My wedding-robe is but a shroud,
   But it is fair and white.
And over me, from head to feet,
They've sprinkled daisies, fresh and sweet.

Away we drift together,
   The moon beneath us shining;
The dark cloud of my life is rent
   And shows its silver lining;
And now I see how much the ore
   Needed its fierce refining.
Below, some weep,—some moan and shiver,—
But I rejoice,—yea, love! forever!

THE LADY PRESIDENT'S BALL.

I.

"THE lights in the President's mansion,
    The gas-lights cheery and red,
I see them glowing and glancing,
    As I toss on my wearisome bed;
I see them gemming the windows,
    And, starlike, studding the hall,
Where the tide of fashion flows inward
    To the Lady President's Ball.

II.

" My temples are throbbing with fever,
    My limbs are palsied with pain;
And the crash of that festal music
    Burns into my aching brain,—
Till I rave with delirious fancies,
    And coffin and bier and pall
Mix up with the flowers and laces
    Of my Lady President's Ball.

III.

" What matter that I, poor private,
    Lie here on my narrow bed,
With the fever scorching my vitals
    And dazing my hapless head?
What matters that nurses are callous,
    And rations meagre and small,
So long as the *beau monde* revel
    At the Lady President's Ball?

IV.

"Who pities my poor old mother?
   Who comforts my sweet young wife?
Alone in the distant city,
   With sorrow sapping their life.
I have no money to send them,
   They cannot come at my call,—
No money? yet hundreds are wasting
   At my Lady President's Ball!

V.

"Hundreds—ay! hundreds of thousands!
   In satins, jewels, and wine;
French dishes for dainty stomachs,
   (While the black broth sickens mine!)
And jellies and fruits and cool ices,
   And fountains that flash as they fall:
Oh, God! for a cup of cold water
   From the Lady President's Ball!

VI.

"Nurse! bring me my uniform ragged,—
   Ah! why did you blow out the light?
Help me up,—though I'm aching and giddy,
   I must go to my dear ones to-night.
Wife! mother! grown weary with waiting,—
   I'm coming,—I'll comfort ye all——!"
And the private sank dead while they reveled
   At my Lady President's Ball.

WHEN THE GREAT REBELLION'S OVER.

Climbed the baby on her knee,
  With an airy, childish grace,
  Prattled in her lovely face:
"When will papa come to me?"
"Papa?" soft the mother cried,—
  "Papa! ah, the naughty rover!
Sweet, my pet, he'll come to thee
  When the great Rebellion's over!"

"Mamma once had rosy cheeks,
  Danced and sang a merry tune;
  Now she rocks me 'neath the moon,
Sits and sighs, but scarcely speaks."
Sad the smile the mother wore:
  "Sweet, mamma has lost her lover;
She will dance and sing no more
  Till the great Rebellion's over.

"Till the hush of peace shall come,
  Like a quiet fall of snow;
  And the gallant troops shall go
Marching back to hearts at home."
"Papa—home?" the baby lisped,
  Balmy-breathed as summer clover:
"Yes, my darling, home at last,
  And the sad Rebellion over."

Entered at the open door,
  While the mother soothed her child,
  One who neither spoke nor smiled,
Standing on the sunny floor.

Wistful eyes met mournful eyes,
   Hope no more may lingering hover;
Ah, poor heart! thou'lt wait in vain
   Till the great Rebellion's over!

Heart, poor heart! too weak to save,
   Vain your tears,—your longings vain;
   Summer winds and summer rain
Beat already on his grave.
From the flag upon his breast,
(Truer breast it ne'er shall cover!)
   From its mouldering colors wet
   With his blood, shall spring beget
   Lily, rose, and violet,
And a wreath of purple clover.
   With the flag upon his breast
They have hid away your lover.
   Weep not, wail not, let him rest.
   Having bravely stood the test,
   He shall rank among the blest
When the great Rebellion's over!

MISCELLANEOUS POEMS.

THE SLEEPER'S SAIL.

" Mother! I've been on the cliffs out yonder,
    Straining my eyes o'er the breakers free,
To the lovely spot where the sun was setting,
    Setting and sinking into the sea.

" The sky was full of the fairest colors,
    Pink and purple and paley green;
With great soft masses of gray and amber,
    And great bright rifts of gold between.

" And all the birds that way were flying,
    Heron and curlew overhead,
With a mighty eagle westward floating,
    Every plume in their pinions red.

" And then I saw it,—the fairy city,
    Far away o'er the waters deep;
Towers and castles and chapels glowing,
    Like blessèd dreams that we see in sleep.

"What is its name?" " Be still, *acushla*
    (Thy hair is wet with the mist, my boy);
Thou hast looked, perchance, on the Tir-na-n'oge,
    Land of eternal youth and joy.

" Out of the sea when the sun is setting,
    It rises golden and fair to view;
No trace of ruin, or change of sorrow,
    No sign of age where all is new.

THE SLEEPER'S SAIL.

" Forever sunny,—forever blooming,—
    Nor cloud nor frost can touch that spot;
Where the happy people are ever roaming,
    The bitter pangs of the past forgot."

" Mother! we've known no end of trouble
    Since the night when father was drowned i' the bay;
The cow lies dead in the poor old stable,
    The black bread fails us day by day.

" Why should we hunger, weep and hunger,
    Your cheeks grow hollow, your hair turn white,
When over the sea to the Tir-na-n'oge,
    In father's boat we can sail to-night?"

"Nay, nay, my boy, lie down and slumber:
    God's ways are dim to human pride;
None dare sail to the Tir-na-n'oge,
    Save those whom angels come to guide."

The lad's dark eyes grew wide and misty,
    The eager flush his cheek forsook;
As he laid him down on his bed of heather
    The wind the crazy cabin shook.

Hunger and cold, and want and sorrow,
    Howled, like wolves, at the broken wall;
But wrapt in the arms of a weary mother,
    The brave young heart forgets them all.

And the gloom melts into a sunset splendor,
    A castled isle in the rosy west,
Where happy souls the shores are thronging,
    Of the golden city of endless rest.

" *None dare sail to the Tir-na-n'oge,*
    Save those whom angels come to guide!"
—In his deep, deep sleep, the little dreamer
    Sees the door of the house set wide;

THE SLEEPER'S SAIL.

And a beckoning shape, vague, tall, and shining,
    With flickering hair in the doorway stands:
The deep eyes draw him—the strange voice calls him—
    While sleep relaxes the mother's hands.

Ah! little she dreams that the gentle patter,
    Her boy's bare feet on the homely floor,
Like the sound of rain on the hawthorn falling,
    Will stir the pulse of her heart no more!

Little she dreams that his clear eyes never
    Again in her face the smile shall seek;
Or his young arms clasp her neck, while ever
    The bright lips warm her withered cheek!

—He feels the salt wind past him rushing,
    The moonlit cliffs are white as snow,
As, step by step, he slowly clambers
    Down to his father's boat below.

How close it seems—the fairy city!—
    More blessed and beauteous than before;
The moonshine, like a bridge of silver,
    Stretching away to its flowery shore.

"What matter if the sail be broken?
    The hands of angels guide my boat;
We'll sing the *Ave Maris Stella*,
    As down the pleasant tide we float.

"O fair and lovely Tir-na-n'oge!
    I see thy castles close at hand;
Thy fragrant winds are wafted o'er me,
    The happy saints are on the strand.

"My father!—is it he? How altered!
    Bright,—strong? Gray-haired and poor no more?
Good angel! hold the boat securely,—
    'Tis but a step,—I'll leap ashore——"

  *   *   *   *   *   *

High on the cliffs the light-house keeper
   Caught the sound of a piercing scream;
Low in her hut the lonely widow
   Moaned in the maze of a troubled dream;

And saw in her sleep a seaman ghostly,
   With sea-weeds clinging in his hair,
Into her room, all wet and dripping,
   A drownèd boy on his bosom bear.

Vainly the light-house keeper lingered,
   And peered, good soul, through the moonlit pane;
Vainly the widow, waking, fingered
   The empty bed where her boy had lain.

Over Death's sea on a bridge of silver
   The child to his Father's arms had passed;
Heaven was nearer than Tir-na-n'oge,
   And the Golden City was reached at last.

UNSEEN YET SEEN.

I HAVE read somewhere in a thoughtful book,
   Of an old cathedral over the sea
(A wonder of art, whose every nook
   Is full of a charming mystery),
That up, high up, on the topmost point
   Of roof and tower and belfry gray,
Which the gracious summer dews anoint,
   And the birds frequent in their airy way:
There are marvels of sculpture, rare and fine,
Flower and fruit and trailing vine;
And lovely angels with folded wings,
Cut from the stone, like living things;

And pure Madonnas, and saints at prayer,
With reverent heads and flowing hair,—
Colossal figures, by height diminished,
With every lineament finely finished.
 Yet all this delicate tracery
  Was not for the eyes of mortal made;
 For none but God and His angels see
  The marvelous sculpture there displayed.

Who was the artist whose chisel wrought
Into exquisite work such exquisite thought?
Why did he labor for years and years,
Through days of travailing, nights of tears,
Under the stars and under the moon,
Dreaming, designing, at morn and noon,
To work these wonders in wood and stone,
Which God and His angels see alone?

God and His angels! Behold the key
To this strange, unworldly mystery!
That grand old artist, mounted on high,
 Like an eagle perched in his eyrie lonely,
Working with hand and heart and eye,
 Was working for God and His angels only.

No mean, self-conscious motive stirred
 The tranquil depths of his patient heart;
But praise or censure, alike unheard,
 In his chaste communings had no part.
Far, far below him the world was spread,
 Like a painted picture, small and dim;
And the voice of creatures, the rush and tread
 Of the mighty millions, were lost on him.
While the skies bent over him, blue and broad,
So full of the awful, unseen God,—
Heaven seemed so near, and earth so far,
No selfish thought could his labor mar.

Ah! what a lovely moral lies
    Hid (like the delicate tracery
    On roof and tower and gray belfry
    Of the old cathedral over the sea)
In its storied legend's dim disguise!

'Tis worth an infinite treasure to know
    (Whatever beside should be unknown)
How utterly false and mean we grow,
    When we work for the eyes of men alone.
How blind and aching our sight becomes,
    With the glare of glory such works may win us,
While a selfish purpose narrows and numbs
    All that is noble and fresh within us.
'Tis only when self is dead and gone,
    And our souls from the mists of passion free,
That the angels of God come in and crown
    Our labors with immortality.

O Artists! who work with pencil or pen,
With chisel or brush, for the praise of men,—
When you fold your hands at the twilight's close,
And muse in your darkened studios,
Do you never consider, once for all,
How that other and deeper night must fall,
When earth and the things thereof shall be
Lost, like a dream, in Eternity?
When, shrinking and startled,—with soul laid bare,—
The creature shall meet the Creator there,
And learn at the foot of the Great White Throne ·
(A truth which should never have been unknown)
That nothing avails us under the sun,
In word or in work, save that which is done
For the honor and glory of God alone?

Oh, blessèd indeed are the pure of heart!
For they shall see God in their glorious art;

And joyous shall be (though the world wax dim),
If none shall behold them save Him, save Him!
And they are the sculptors whose works shall last,
   Whose names shall shine as the stars on high,
When deep in the dust of a ruined past
   The labors of selfish souls shall lie.

Brothers! who work with pencil or pen,
With chisel or brush, for the praise of men,
   Whate'er ye design, whatever ye do,
Seek first the kingdom of God,—and then
   All else shall be graciously added to you.
And the moral is yours, which was sent to me
From the old cathedral over the sea.

LOST LEWIE.

I.

With shining blossoms on his bosom flung,
   With waxen lids weighed down in slumber sweet;
The spell of silence on his merry tongue,
   And on his dancing feet;
Let the hot tears drop burning on his brow,
    He cannot feel them now.

II.

He cannot open wide those lustrous eyes,
   Whose jetty lashes shade the marble cheek;
The rose has faded on his lips of ice,
   He does not smile or speak;
Kiss his small mouth,—no bubbling laugh comes out,
    No boyish, mirthful shout.

III.

Yet while the light of waxen tapers falls
    Upon his tiny form, so mute, so white,
Beyond the posterns of the heavenly walls
    The boy stands glad and bright;
And while we shroud our eyes and weep and moan,
    He kneels before the Throne:

IV.

Kneels with his dark, bright eyes, like stars, aglow,
    His young face rosy with celestial bloom;
No shadow on his brow or robes of snow,
    To tell us of the tomb.
Pain, Death, and Woe? He hath exchanged all three
    For Immortality!

V.

Sweet Lew! young hero. Frank and fearless Lew!
    Wild as the bird that knows no caged control,
Your spirit was too brave, your heart too true,
    Too pure your childish soul,
To live and drain this cup of gall and strife,
    Which men call human life:

VI.

To live and breathe this tainted atmosphere,
    In which high aims are low, and low ones high;
In which the best of us, from year to year,
    Our frailties multiply;
Or fall through weakness or through reckless daring,
    To die at last despairing.

VII.

Ah, God be praised, dear Lew ! that in His time,
   His own good time, the gentle angels came
To waft you softly to the changeless clime,
   That knows no sin or shame ;
To place you joyous on the Shepherd's knee,
     Safe from all misery.

VIII.

Oh, little face, that seest things divine !
   Oh, little suffering hands, upraised in bliss !
Oh, little well-known form in raiment fine !
   Oh, child we long to kiss !
Sing, from your happy heart, your rapturous song
     Among the angel throng !

IX.

Though you may never more make merry here,
   With earthly little ones or earthly toys ;
Though mamma miss your step upon the stair,
   And the dear papa miss your happy noise,—
And little sister, prattling, ask each day
     Why Lewie stays away—

X.

Yet, darling child, we would not call you back,
   We would not rob you of your new-born joy;
Smiles *we* may thirst for,—laughing prattle lack,
   But heaven is yours, sweet boy !
Fold up the dress, put by the well-worn shoe ;
   God's arms are round him in a close embrace,
   God's face bends smiling to his radiant face,—
     'Tis well with little Lew.

A RED-LETTER DAY.

THERE is a little picture framed in sweet forget-me-nots,
Which fills within my memory the cosiest of spots;

It nestles where the sunlight comes, the earliest and the last;
It is the record of a Day, the dearest in the past.

A little quiet room within a cottage on the hill
(The very home of Heaven's peace, secluded, warm, and still).

A veil-like mist, a wind without that waves the leaves apart,
No sunlight in the heavy sky, but much within the heart.

There, from the windows broad and deep, we see the chapel spire,
And one dear friend sits in our midst and stirs the blazing fire.

The meek Madonna on the wall with angels at her feet,
The glowing hearth,—the chairs set round,—make comfort so complete,

That while old books are strewn about, and older friends are nigh,
We think not of the clouds without, or winds that wail and sigh.

But sitting there, we read, or play a quiet game of whist,
Till Time puts on such silent wings, his flight is scarcely missed.

And underneath, and in between, a cheery monotone,
The tide of talk and laughter low flows ever on and on.

Kind thoughts and pleasant repartee; quotations, odd and
    quaint,
Flow ever on, till in the room the light grows soft and
    faint.

Then with a smile and sigh we say (turning to that dear
    friend):
"This has been one sweet happy day, and now it has an
    end."

Then through the veil-like mist we go, and through the
    shadows late,
And, looking back, we pause to watch that dear friend at
    the gate.

This is the little picture framed in sweet forget-me-nots,
That fills within my memory the cosiest of spots;

That nestles where the sunlight comes, the earliest and the
    last,
That is the record of a Day, the dearest in the past.

IN THE VINTAGE.

When the autumn sun was sinking low,
    And the crimson clouds took many shapes,
I stood in the vineyard long ago,
    Gathering up the grapes.
The young Bianca at my side,
    With a sun-flush on her braided hair,
And her slender fingers, purple-dyed,
    Wrought singing softly there.

Between the snatches of her song
    (While the crimson clouds grew pale and numb),

IN THE VINTAGE.

We talked of the pleasant home to be
   In the pleasant years to come;
The thousand tender hopes that Love
   Doth joy to crown and throne within
The sacred court of future years,
   We joyed to fashion then.
And when the young moon peered between
   The waving branches dim and gray,
I left Bianca at the gate,
   And singing, went away.

Alas! that we dream a dream, and wake
   To find the vision dead and dumb!
Alas! that those royal hopes should be
   Clay in the years to come!
When the autumn sun again sunk low,
   And the crimson clouds took many shapes,
I stood in the vineyard, love-bereft,
   Gathering up the grapes.
The twilight eyes and the wild-rose cheek
   Of my fragile love no more were there:
Nor the broken snatches of pleasant song
   Thrilling the quiet air.
Need there was none a nest to build,
   When the lost, lost bird no nest might share.

I did not moan, I did not wail,
   I did not call her back to me;
For dark was the gulf,—but the shore beyond
   Was brighter than earth could be.
Brighter than earth, with its vineyards vast
   Where the Sun in its glory ne'er declines,
And the tranquil forms of the blest repose
   Under the purple vines.
And where my love (while the incense warm,
   Like a misty veil, her tresses drapes)

Goeth with timid steps and slow
    Gathering the Master's grapes.
The olden love from her pleasant eyes
    Drippeth, like sweet rain, down on me;
And her brow is writ with the solemn lore
    Of her immortality!

And though, when the withered leaves without
    Are all in the restless wind astir,
I sometimes sit in my closet dim,
    And dream of the life that might have been
If God had spared me her,
    I know, ere the twilight over the hill
With another autumn sun escapes,
    I shall go with my love through the viewless land,
And gather the Master's grapes.

THE SKELETON AT THE FEAST.

I.

BRIGHT glows the fire in the stately rooms,
    Soft gleams the light on statues,—vases rare,—
Carpets and curtains from the Eastern looms,
    Mirrors and ottomans of damask fair;
But in the midst a plaintive voice is heard;
    A chilly shadow deepens o'er the spot;
The very air is vibrant with the words:
    "I was a stranger, and ye heeded not!"

II.

Heap up the grate with generous anthracite,
    (Full cheerily the plate and crystal shine!)

Spread out the banquet in the rosy light;
  Bid the old butler bring his choicest wine.
In vain,—in vain,—ye cannot shut it out,
  Shadow and voice are mightier than ye think:—
" I was a-hungered and ye fed Me not;
  A-thirsty, and ye gave Me not to drink!"

III.

Fill up the goblets with the golden wine,
  And pledge this blushing beauty in the glass.
Ha! how her emeralds and diamonds shine,
  Like drops of early dew on summer grass!
Ha! in her royal velvets without peer,
  Her cheek beneath her jeweled hair grows hot.
What! shivering, *ma belle?* What dost thou hear?—
  " I was a-naked and ye clothed Me not!"

IV.

But this is folly. Bid the music sound.
  ('Tis time these whining beggars should have ceased!)
Hither, ye merry dancers,—while the ground
  Glows with the dying flowers of the feast.
Wind in and out,—glide up and down; be quick!
  We'll reel and revel till the day breaks fair.
Shrill-piercing through the din,—hist!—" I was sick,—
  Sick, and in prison, and ye came not there!"

V.

Avenging God! the brilliant room grows dark,—
  The blushing beauties grin as fleshless bones!
Mildew and worm attack the feast; and hark!
  The pleading Voice now speaks in judgment-tones:

"Depart from Me, ye cursed, into the flame
    Lit for the damned from all eternity.
For inasmuch as ye did not this same
    Unto My poor, ye did it not to Me!"

"HIC JACET."

THE MATERIALIST'S REMORSE.

O PURE and pale! O pale and calm!
    O restful corse within the mould,
With meek dead eyes and idle palm,
    And raiment strangely cold!

How faith grows weak amid the gloom
    That curtains in thy pallid rest!
And hope, like summer's fragile bloom,
    Is shivered on thy breast.

But love, alone, in thine eclipse,
    Is not a-tremble nor apart:
But lays her lips to thy cold lips,
    Her heart to thy still heart.

Oh let it thrill thy pulseless frame,
    Oh let it stain thy pallid cheek,
Fill up thy hollow eyes with flame,
    And then—arise and speak!

It may not be. Through the still night
    The wind sails sighing from the moon;
The stars are shedding tears of light
    That thou hast died so soon.

And with the night-dew in my hair,
   And purple pansies at my feet,
I wrap me in my dull despair,
   As in a winding-sheet.

For not a clod lies on thy heart,
   As heavy as this lonely weight
Which bows me down, and forms a part
   Of my resistless fate.

The moonlight shivers down the path,
   The trees in ruddy blossoms bleed,—
O Death, thy solemn after math
   Is sad and sere indeed!

SONG OF THE SNOW-BIRD.

I come when the heavens are white and still,
   And the winds blow from the north;
When the echoes are sharp by the frozen rill,
   And the little ones go not forth.

I wander untamed through the bracing air,
   I and my fellows free,
Picking up crumbs where the soil seems bare,
   And chirping of snows to be;

Of the soft light flakes that shall flutter down,
   Till their coming is fast and dense,
And they whiten the eaves of the cottage brown
   And bury the wayside fence;

Of the wreaths that shall hang over latchless doors,
    To startle the poor incomer;
Of the sheets that shall stretch over bleak, wild moors,
    And cover the corpse of Summer.

Merry, I tap at the window low
    Of some pleasant valley cot,
Where the shadows of children sway to and fro,
    And the cold or the frost come not;

Where the firelight flickers o'er mouths of mirth,
    Or leaps to the friendly eyes;
Where the mother sits close by the cosy hearth,
    And the babe in the cradle lies.

And I tap, I tap, till the little ones come
    To peer through the frosty pane,
And tempt me to nibble the proffered crumb,
    But tempt me to enter in vain.

For down from the heavens so still and dim,
    To the earth so still below,
Like frozen foam from a goblet's brim,
    Droppeth the pleasant snow.

And mad with the mirth of the dancing things
    My birdlings love the best,
I scatter the flakes with my russet wings
    And flee to my far-off nest.

MOTHER'S CORNER.

In the ruddiest glow of the western light
    She sits in her favorite nook:
The dear hands busy, the dear face clothed
    With its tender mother-look.
The smile that softens the quiet mouth
    No evil pang embitters;
And the sunlight touches the fingers deft,
    Till the thimble gleams and glitters.

O the tranquil moon of the mother-life
    That sways our human tide;
How the household good and the household ill
    In her slender hands abide!
'Tis a little ripple of broken toys,
    Or the wreck of a strong existence;
'Tis a timid yearning of childish mouths,
    Or a deep cry in the distance.

'Tis the clinging clasp of a baby's hand,
    Or the kiss of the new-made bride;
Or the groping wail of the last white one
    Who turned to the wall, and died.
Little or great, she meets them all,
    With the seal of her trust upon her;
And the sobs are stilled, and the tears are dried,
    In the light of the mother's corner.

Alas! for the homes where the bride must wait,
    And the strong man cry in vain;
Where the sick one turns to the vacant chair,
    And dies in his unsoothed pain.

No tender touch from the quiet lips,
   No balm for the heart-pierced mourner;
O Christ! by the cottage of Nazareth!
   Despoil not *our* mother's corner!

THE TWILIGHT FAIRY.

When the lights of the autumn noon flicker and fade,
   And the gloaming comes solemnly down,
A fair little face on my bosom is laid,
   Half hidden in tresses of brown.

Two shining arms circle my neck in their play,
   Sweet words from the merry lips blow,
The old fire crackles, the dim shadows sway,
   And the wind at the lattice is low.

And brushing the hair from the pure childish brow,
   And hushing the sweet-singing tongue,
I tell of the mother who died long ago,
   When the years of my manhood were young.

How she lay 'mid the pillows, divested of bloom,
   Her thin fingers crossed on her breast,
While the wind, like a banshee, wailed into the room,
   And the sun-flush went out in the west.

How the nurse, in the twilight, brought softly to me
   The babe of my beautiful dead,—
The gay little fairy who sits on my knee
   And lists to the words that are said.

And I tell how I caught her, and tenderly laid
    Her head on my bosom as now,
While the old fire crackled, the dim shadows swayed,
    And the wind at the lattice was low.

And the lips of my darling grow rosy with smiles
    When I speak of the baby in white,
With its fat, foolish fingers and wonderful eyes,
    Crushed down on my bosom that night;

But the thought of the mother who sleeps in the years
    Seems something so softly divine,
That the eyes of my darling grow misty with tears,
    And her little heart throbs against mine.

Thus we sit in the twilight, uncertain and vast,
    Till the embers drop down at our feet;
And we talk of the future, the present, the past,
    In a monotone tender and sweet.

The portrait that hangs o'er the dim mantel-shelf,
    With hair round the girlish face blown,
Smiles down on that miniature type of itself,
    And on me,—as we sit there alone.

And I think, yes, I think of that pitiful day
    When these beautiful twilights must end;
When the embers will crackle, the shadows will sway,
    But my fairy will miss her old friend!

When the seat at the fireside vacant shall be,
    And the lips from their legends shall rest;
When the light form shall slip from the weary old knee,
    And the head from the weary old breast.

Oh, the roses and grass-flowers out of my clay
    By the breath of the spring shall be blown!
But who will take heed of my darling that day,
    When she weeps in the silence alone?

CALLED AND CHOSEN.

I.

STILL runs the river past the broken wall
    Where Claude and I were wont to sit of old,
Watching the limpid waters slide and fall
    Over the dam,—a sheet of molten gold;
What time the clouds, like fairies gayly dressed,
Built up their glorious castles in the west;

II.

Our sketch-books idly open on our knees,
    The smell of wall-flowers filling all the air;
'Twas dreamy joy to watch whole argosies
    Of gorgeous dragon-flies make shipwreck there;
And bees go diving with their foolish heads
    Into intoxicating lily-beds.

III.

"Sweet idleness!" said Claude; and then he drew
    His smiling lips into a graver line,
And looked out with his earnest eyes of blue
    To where the rosy river ran like wine:
"O purple-dragon-flies! O golden bees!
To you belongs this life of summer ease,—

IV.

But not to me"—and then his face grew broad
    With purest purpose, and his eyes gave out
Great placid rays, as if the stars of God
    Within their azure heaven wheeled about:—
"Except a man deny himself," he said;
And then broke off, and drooped his classic head.

V.

Again: "The kingdom suffers violence,
   And naught save violence shall win the prize;
Dost comprehend, dear heart, the mystic sense?"
   I shivered, as with cold, and hid mine eyes;
And all the glorious skies and glowing stream
Swept into shadow, like a broken dream.

VI.

That was five years ago. To-day, beside
   The ruined wall, I sit alone and study
The same rich sunset clouds, the same swift tide,
   Glassing the mill-dam with its ripples ruddy;
But on my lap, 'twixt folded hands, there lies
An open letter, traced 'neath foreign skies.

VII.

Dominican and priest, where Lacordaire's
   First white-robed friars preached and prayed and read,
He that was Claude, now Father Saint Pierre,
   Speaks from the written page as from the dead:
And, joyous as a lover at the tryst,
Sighs ardently to shed his blood for Christ.

VIII.

O happy Claude! O happier Saint Pierre!
   O happiest of all the souls that take
The cross of self-denial up, and bear
   It bravely to the end for Christ's sweet sake!
Sail on, gay dragon-flies! hum on, bright bees!
We envy not your life of honeyed ease.

THE POET'S LITTLE RIVAL.

A DAINTY desk of rosewood,
   With a half-completed sonnet,
And a bunch of summer roses
   In a Sêvres vase upon it;
And a bronze and crystal standish,
   And a golden pen or two;
Whole reams of satin paper,—
   Pink and azure and *écru:*
And the poets, great and tiny,
   Scattered round in gold and blue.

On the wall a linnet singing,
   At the desk a deep *fauteuil*,
Under-foot an Indian matting;
   And the casement, low and cool,
Twined about with waving ivy
   Where the sunset glory burns,
And the light and shade go creeping,
   Making bright and dark, by turns,
The pendent basket swinging
   From the trellis, full of ferns.

And the poet, ah, the poet!
   He quits his pleasant seat,
And sees his little daughter
   In the garden at his feet:
Walking with her fair-haired mother,
   In a dress of snowy lawn,
Prattling softly to the flowers,
   As they wander on and on;
Saying: "I must make a poem
   Ere the roses all are gone!"

Then the poet leans and listens
    With a quaint and tender air,
As the bird-like child goes darting
    Through the beautiful parterre.
"Bravo! bravo! little poet!"
    (Startled, flushed with love's sunshine :)
"See my poem, papa darling!
    Every word a blossom fine."
"Sweet," he says; "God bless thee, daughter;
    Ne'er was poem writ like thine!"

MISUNDERSTANDINGS.

How like unsightly worms they ceaseless crawl
    Under the pleasant roses of our lives,
Gnawing and gnawing, till the fresh leaves fall,
    And nothing green or beautiful survives!

Leaving a ruin of corroding slime
    That which was fair and wholesome just before;
Ah, tell us not new buds will blow in time!
    These precious plants will never blossom more.

Now 'tis a false report; anon, a glance,
    Sidelong, but with no secret malice fraught:
We press our hearts, as though a poisoned lance
    Had pierced them, and a bleeding fissure wrought.

Then 'tis a chain of trifles (as we think),
    Lighter than feathers blown into the air,—
But when rude hands have forged them link by link,
    We clank our iron fetters in despair.

And straightway, 'twixt our own and some dear heart,
   A nameless, viewless barrier is set;
And lives, long mingled, flow, thenceforth, apart
   Unto one common ocean of regret.

And though we strove to carve, as sculptors do,
   Our stony trials into shapes serene,
Our noblest image of the Pure and True
   Would be, just then, denounced as base and mean.

Ah, it is hard to hold our souls in peace,
   To keep our spirits sunny, while these things
Haunt us, like evil birds, and never cease
   Making the sunshine dusky with their wings!

But there is One who understands it all:
   The Wounded Heart that 'neath the olive-trees,
And on the Mount, in bitterness let fall
   The secret of Its own vast agonies.

And we may trust our faults and failures, too,
   Unto His love, as humble children should;
Content that if all others misconstrue,
   By Him, at least, our hearts are understood.

PASSING FOOTSTEPS.

I sit in my room and listen to the feet that hurry on,
Through the street, beneath my window, from darkness unto dawn.

From dawn unto the darkness, like the sound when the tide is high,
Like the sound of the autumn forests, those footsteps rustle by.

And I've learned to pause in my studies, and bend with a listening ear,
When, through the rush of the many, some well-known feet I hear.

I never have seen their faces, I never have heard their speech,
Yet my heart has a magic mirror with the face and the form of each.

One, through the crowd, goes lightly, the step of a little child,
That walks with its guardian angel, in raiment undefiled.

And I close my book when I hear it, for the Past, like a velvet door,
Swings back on its noiseless hinges, and I look on the lost once more.

There are vistas of light and fragrance, there are fountains with silver rain,
And the fresh winds blow from the long ago, and my heart is a child's again!

Another, I know, is a maiden's, by the footstep's airy grace,
So I turn to my magic mirror and gaze on her flitting face.

'Tis the face of a vagrant Peri, with the deep eyes of the South,
And the rose that the bulbul worships is ripe in her sunny mouth.

I smile on her forehead's whiteness, on her cheek's quick-coming red,
And I sigh: "God bless thee, maiden, for thou mind'st me of my dead!"

One other foot, through the shadows, goes by, and I list again:
'Tis the step of a man grown aged among his fellow-men;

'Tis a heavy, halting footstep,—and my glass has a dim eclipse,—
A sad, old face, with a patient eye, bent brow, and trembling lips.

'Tis a weary while since a mother first guided those stumbling feet,
They have grown unfit for this busy mart where the world's strong pulses beat;

But out where the grasses murmur, and the meadows stretch away,
In the sunshine and the silence they should rest or, peaceful, stray.

Oh, my heart, like a sea storm-swollen, its spray to my eyes upsends,
And I weep for the aged stranger who knows no home or friends.

Till out of my grief's deep ocean this thought is Venus-born,
That, free of the curtaining shadows that stretch from dusk to morn,

The way of those many footsteps, the street-way long and broad,
Through the gates of the glorious city may lead to the throne of God!

And I see the pilgrims going, white-robed and laurel-crowned,
Where the light throbs down from the face of Christ, and the angels stand around:

The lily child and its guardian, the maid and the stranger hoar,
They are all in the shining circle,—they are blest for evermore!

—I sit in my room and listen to the restless tide without;
But my magic mirror is shivered, and my lamp has flickered out.

THE QUEEN'S EPITAPH.

I.

DID she say unto her minstrels: "Sing my fame to listening time"?
Did she say unto her poets: "Write my praise in silver rhyme"?
To her sculptors did she utter, with a right majestic air:
  "Straightway hasten to prepare
  For my tomb a statue fair,
Carven out of costly marble, with an epitaph sublime;

II.

"Golden sceptre in my fingers, on my head a golden crown,
And a cloak of chiseled ermine from my shoulders dropping down:
'*Eleanore, King Henry's consort,*' be it jeweled in the stone,
    '*Fairest queen that ever shone,*
    Star-like, on the English throne,
While the flower of Norman knighthood kissed the border of her gown'?"

III.

Heaven forgive the foul suspicion of the dead queen's lowliness!
Gentle saint, forgive the satire of thy soul's supreme distress!
Wailing feebly: "O my maidens, O my courtiers, let no hand
    To my memory in the land
    Raise a mausoleum grand,
But upon my tomb write simply: '*Eleanore, la pecheresse*'!"

IV.

Oh, the depths of purest wisdom those few gasping words express!
Sunset clouds of rose and amber, clad in twilight's sober dress,
Sunset clouds of royal splendor o'er her death-bed taking wing:
    Stripped of sceptre, crown, and ring,
    Face to face with Christ the King,
ELEANORE LA REINE was lost in ELEANORE LA PECHERESSE!

FRANK, MY DARLING!

How heavenly calm the soul looks out
  From baby's azure eyes!
As pure and fair, as clear and sweet,
As the stream that flows through the golden street,
  And waters Paradise.

Haply the flowers of that bright land,
  Where fadeless verdure grows,
Brighten anew in his dewy lips,
On his shining shoulders and finger-tips,
  In his cheek's delicious rose.

And verily those who brightest bathe
  Their wings in shadeless light,
The souls of children who perished pure,
In their early youth, and were caught secure
  From the touch of coming blight,—

Verily they their God must thank,
  And smile, as they float afar,
To see 'mid these world-weeds, dark and dank,
The stainless soul of our baby Frank
  Shine out like a sister star.

O happy darling! I clasp thee close,
  I clasp thee faint with fear;
For, looking into thy liquid eyes,
I hear the rustle of Paradise,
  And feel the angels near.

And I hide thee in my bosom, babe,
  I kiss thee o'er and o'er,

Lest the angels catch thee, as if in play,
Out of my arms in happy play,
And bear thee away—away—away,—
   To bring thee back no more!

Many a darling fair as thou,
   From mother's breast as fond,
Has floated away with the placid dead,
Through the pearly gates, by the angels led,
   To swell the ranks beyond.

And blessèd are they, I know full well,
   For they rest and know no sin;
And the bowers of Heaven are bright: and they
May drink with their innocent lips, alway,
   The waters that gush therein.

Yet, if God wills, lead not our boy
   Where that air river rolls!
His little sparkling life would be
Only a drop in eternity,—
A drop in your rich eternity,
   Replete with glorious souls!

You—you can spare him yet awhile,
   Your court shall lessen never;
But we, ah, woe! how could we rest,
With empty arms and yearning breast,
By night—by day,—how could we rest,
   And miss our babe forever?

FIAT VOLUNTAS DEI.

Once I made plans, and said: When spring-tide rains
   Have made the summer bloom, I'll dream my dream;
And when the autumn garners in its grain,
And ere the winter whitens all the plain,
   I will fulfill my long-projected scheme.

But, ah! (heigh-ho!) before the silvery rains
   Melted in bloom, my dream was sacrificed:
And autumn proved my schemes were worse than vain;
And all the winter, in a vice of pain,
   My heart was caught and crushed and agonized.

Sufficient for the day—O Lord supreme!
   Thy lips have said—*shall be the ill thereof;*
And now I have no plans, I make no schemes,
But, like an infant rocked in tranquil dreams,
   Within Thine arms I simply trust and love.

LIGHT IN DARKNESS.

The sunlight, through the western windows stealing,
   Fretted with gold the dim cathedral gloom,
   Where, in the shadow of an ancient tomb,
      A little child was kneeling.

All other worshipers had gone away:
   The air was fragrant with the last sweet hymn;
   The sanctuary lamp was burning dim,
      And slowly waned the day.

LIGHT IN DARKNESS.

Still knelt the child; the sunlight stooped to win
   A golden lustre from her tresses brown,
   And in her patient eyes looked sadly down,
      To find no sight within.

Blind and alone! A melancholy lot!
   To know of birds and blushing flowers without,
   Of pleasant skies and trees that waved about,
      And yet to see them not!

Kneeling, she prayed: " Lord Jesus, God of kindness,
   Who, in Thy human dwelling undefiled,
   Hast known and felt the sorrows of a child,
      Have pity on my blindness!

" My little day of life doth wane apace;
   The earth's fair glories I may never see;
   I have no love within my heart save Thee,
      Oh, let me see Thy face!"

Her head sank down; the rippling hair, unbound,
   Fell, like a veil, athwart her pallid cheek;
   The lips, all tremulous, had ceased to speak,
      And shadows settled round.

But, all the long night through, the pillared gloom
   Was lightened by the flash of angel wings;
   And angel voices made low murmurings
      Around that ancient tomb.

And when the morn from out the dewy east
   Came, in her jewels, like a blushing bride,
   The heavy chancel doors were opened wide
      To acolyte and priest.

And they, who gathered at the matins there,
  Found in the shadow of the tomb antique
  A fair, dead figure with a marble cheek,
    And fingers locked in prayer.

Stooping, they wreathed the lily on her brow;
  But, as they bore her to the bier away,
  They sang: " Hosanna to the Lord this day:
    The blind one seeth now!"

SAINT MARTIN'S SUMMER.

The gentle sound of dropping leaves
  Is soothing as a psalm,
As down I stray through pleasant fields,
  Replete with autumn balm.

The fine perspective, blue with haze
  (As soft as silken fleece),
Seen through the rainbow-tinted trees,
  Is full of golden peace.

And, like a picture in a frame
  Of scarlet leaves, I see
Saint Martin at the Amiens gate,
  In ancient Picardy,

Bestowing (with that tender grace
  Which knightly faith awoke)
Upon a shivering beggar-maid
  His warm and costly cloak.

SAINT MARTIN'S SUMMER.

O love of God! which doth outlast
    All change and all decay,
Methinks the legend of the past
    Repeats itself to-day.

For where the woodland, bare and sere,
    Flames, like a dying fire,
The shivering beggar of the year
    Hath found Saint Martin's tire.

And, with a blush upon her cheek,
    Lax-limbed, as one who dozes,
She basks beside the sunny creek,
    And dreams of summer roses.

Father! who shedd'st so ripe a glow
    O'er nature's wasted presence,
Make the late autumn of our lives
    Bloom with such mellow pleasance;

That when the soul's October rains
    Have washed all radiance from her,
One glorious gain may still remain,
    —Saint Martin's golden summer!

THE FATE OF THE FAIRY SWAN.

A note prefixed by Moore to his pathetic song, "*Silent, O Moyle! be the voice of thy waters!*" will explain this little poem.

"Fionnuala, the daughter of Lir, was by some supernatural power transformed into a swan, and condemned to wander for many hundred years over certain lakes and rivers of Ireland, till the coming of Christianity, when the first sound of the Mass-bell was to be the signal of her release."

This fanciful fiction (typical, no doubt, of the release of the soul through the agency of the Gospel from the dark thraldom of superstition) was found among the manuscript translations from the Irish in the possession of the late Countess of Moira.

"When shall the swan, her death-note singing,
Sleep with wings in darkness furled?
When shall heaven, its sweet bell ringing,
Call my spirit from this stormy world?"—SONG OF FIONNUALA.

I.

UP and down the crystal river
Sailed the fair enchanted swan;
In the east, a rose-flush quivered,
In the west, the stars grew wan;
On the bank in costume rude
Knelt a mighty multitude.

II.

And the dew in gentle showers
Bathed the bishop's cope and crook:
Gemmed the altar crowned with flowers,
Flashed on chalice, bell, and book;
While the priest upon the grass
Offered up the first great Mass.

III.

First great Mass on Erin's altars!
Sunburst brighter than the dawn!

Closer to the reeds and rushes
  Swam the fair enchanted swan;
    Throbbing fast and drooping low,
    Feathered breast and wings of snow.

IV.

With her weird bright eyes she watched them,
  That mysterious multitude,—
Prostrate on the ground, and sobbing,
  As they beat their breasts subdued:
    Every lip (unshorn or bare)
    Trembling with ecstatic prayer.

V.

"Sanctus! Sanctus! Sanctus!" murmured
  At the shrine the bending priest.
All was still,—the very breathing
  Of that mighty gathering ceased,—
    As upon the hush there fell
    Silvery tinkling of a bell!

VI.

Sacred sound, so long awaited!
  Blessèd chiming, long deferred!
In the mist among the rushes
  Something white and trembling stirred,
    As the bird in rapture strong
    Sang her last delicious song:

VII.

"Farewell! Erin, 'mid the waters,
  Shining, like an emerald green,
Ne'er again shall Fionnuala
  On your sparkling lakes be seen;
    After ages of unrest,
    Sweet shall be her slumbers blest.

VIII.

"Christ has triumphed! Christ has riven
  From my soul its shackles sore;
Farewell, Erin! child of heaven!
  Never shall I see thee more.
    Chime, O chime, thou holy bell!
    Lir's lone daughter breathes—farewell!"

IX.

Ringing sweetly, ringing softly,—
  Lo! a white ethereal shape,
With the last clear note of triumph,
  Winged to heaven its glad escape.
    Farewell, lake! Farewell, bright river!
    Fionnuala is free forever!

FEAST OF THE PRESENTATION.

AN ANCIENT TRADITION OF THE MOTHER OF OUR LORD.

THE light slants down the Temple-stair
Upon an aged couple there,
With quiet eyes and silvery hair.

Between them, like a rosebud bright,
And fresh and sweet, a child in white
On either side a hand holds tight.

She hath but three sweet summers told,
That little girl with locks of gold,
Between her parents grave and old;

Yet round her hidden angels say:
"*Gloria tibi, Domine!*
Our sovereign Queen is here to-day!"

And while she marvels at the hymn,
Sweet Anne and gentle Joachim
Conduct her up the staircase dim.

The Golden Gate is open wide,
And, in and out, a surging tide,
The groups of strangers ceaselessly glide.

But no one heeds the aged pair,
Or the infant with her sunny hair
(God's favorite friends forgotten fare).

And few behold the high-priest stand
In his glittering vestments, old and grand,
With unrolled parchment in his hand,

Save little Mary, brave and sweet,
Who kneels before the Rabbi's feet
And lisps the words his lips repeat.

She does not say: "O gracious King!
I'm but a little trembling thing,
Too weak to quit my mother's wing!"

She does not plead: "O Lord divine!
Forbear, until I taste the wine
Of future joys which may be mine!"

Nor still with cheeks and eyelids wet:
"My harvest is not ripened yet,
My zeal is mastered by regret!"

But, firm and free and strong of nerve
(While radiant smiles the bright lips curve):
"Take all, O God! without reserve!"

And Anna feels her heart grow weak,
And Joachim is pale of cheek,
As the maiden, rising, turns to speak.

She stands between them, like a lamb,
She gives to each a tiny palm:
And says "Farewell!" in accents calm.

And then it seems as dark as night,
As the Levite takes the child in white
And leads her slowly from their sight.

O latticed doors! which ope and close.
Upon that tiny, virgin rose,
Ye could not hide her if ye chose!

O Temple walls! which stretch away
Majestic, in the golden day,
Ye cannot shut *her* in for aye!

For lo! her glory shall flame forth
Throughout the south, throughout the north,
And in the west,—where God is wroth.

And through the east shall ring her name,
And Mahomet himself proclaim
In these mysterious words her fame:

"*Speak Koran! tell how Mary, wise,
Entered the temple at sunrise,
And veiled herself from mortal eyes!*"

O Joachim! O Anna, mild!
O parents of the undefiled!
Resign with joy that chosen child.

For safe behind the latticed screen
She shall grow up, by men unseen,
A lily, pure and most serene.

And angels shall her playmates be,
To guard the maiden on whose knee
Shall bloom the' Incarnate Deity.

And after her (the prophets sing),—
Shall eager virgins following
Be brought with gladness to the King!

IN MEMORIAM.

REV. FELIX JOSEPH BARBELIN.

I.

FATHER and friend! shepherd of many lambs!
  Is it too late for *this* one to draw near,
And drop from out her prayer-enfolded palms
  The flowers of saddest song upon thy bier?
    Out of the distant West in spirit come,
    To kneel beside thee tremulous and dumb?

II.

That crowded church,—how well my fancy paints
  Its sombre drapery, its solemn light!
And in the midst a visage, like a saint's,
  Shining from out the shadows pure and white;
    The dear old hands, like lilies, laid at rest
    Beneath the crucifix upon his breast.

III.

That meek, good face,—'mid children still a child's,—
  The smile upon it was forever young;
And well *they* loved his accents soft and mild,
  The broken music of his foreign tongue;

The serpent's guile, the innocence of dove,
Mingling forever in its zealous love.

IV.

His heart was with them: from the baptized babe
  Up to the stripling and the maiden fair;
His mission lay among the little ones
  Whom Christ committed to His Spouse's care;
    And how he did his work—how long and well
    He labored—let Saint Joseph's children tell!

V.

Early and late, through sunshine and through storm,
  In the tribunal, at the altar-rail,
For thirty years his dear familiar form,
  His pleasant face with suffering often pale,
    Went to and fro, in guise of common things,
    Doing an angel's work on tireless wings.

VI.

Who that has heard his Mass—who that has knelt
  In the confessional and heard his voice
Pleading God's cause so sweetly—but has felt
  A secret thrill which made his heart rejoice?
    And, going forth, has breathed a sunnier air,
    As though our Lord Himself had spoken there!

VII.

Ah! how we'll miss him, who was ever found
  Ready to sympathize and strong to guide!
Ah! how we'll miss him as the years roll round,
  And life grows stern and griefs are multiplied!
    How often yearn, 'mid vexing cares, to be
    Children, to tell our story at his knee!

VIII.

Advent and Christmas we shall, thronging, meet
  To seek our friend 'mid Bethlehem's delights;
And through the Lent, the crowded, close Retreat,—
  We'll miss his reading of the prayers o' nights;
    And when the words of final blessing sound,
    Full many a secret tear will dew the ground.

IX.

May-time will come, and twinkling lights will shine,
  And flower and incense fill the air with balm;
But one dear visage at that blessèd shrine
  Will look no more upon us, meek and calm.
    And other hands than his will then dispense
    The First Communion to the innocents.

X.

Lo! in the octave of the Sacred Heart,
  He sought his refuge in that school of peace;
Take him, O Lord! all-loving as Thou art,
  Clad in the raiment of his fresh release;
    Take him and fold him there in deathless bliss,
    And may *our* latter end be like to his!

THE END.

www.ingramcontent.com/pod-product-compliance
Lightning Source LLC
Chambersburg PA
CBHW020151170426
43199CB00010B/980